MORE PRAISE FOR *EMBRACING AUTISM*

"The voices here confirm what I've always suspected: everyone is part of one large continuum, and the approaches and insights recounted here can help any parent, any educator, any person deal with any child—or, for that matter, any other person—more effectively and with more compassion. I only wish I'd encountered earlier this cadre of experienced and caring individuals whose humor and resourcefulness represent clearly how best to love and nurture a child."

—CYNTHIA NITZ RIS, J.D., PH.D.,
UNIVERSITY OF CINCINNATI

"A rare, engaging look at individuals with autism and those who love and care for them. Each of these warm, lively accounts educates and entertains. Thoroughly engrossing."

—MARTI LEIMBACH,
AUTHOR OF *DANIEL ISN'T TALKING*

"An inspiring, riveting must-read for parents of children with autism and for anyone who aspires to more meaningful communication with the autistic among us, the brilliant late-talkers and non-talkers who may one day save the world."

—ANNABEL STEHLI,
AUTHOR OF *SOUND OF A MIRACLE,*
A MOTHER'S FIGHT TO FREE HER CHILD FROM AUTISM

"Written by and for parents, educators, and people with autism spectrum disorders (ASD), this book is a compilation of wise, loving, sensitive, and hopeful stories. This thoughtful advice from those who know will be useful for people who care about someone of any age with ASD."

—ROBERT L. HENDREN,
EXECUTIVE DIRECTOR, M.I.N.D. INSTITUTE, UC DAVIS

"What a joy to read! There is, perhaps, no better way to learn about autism than to pay attention to the experiences of those living with it. This collection of stories from people with autism and their families, friends, and colleagues shows a side of autism we don't hear enough about. The authors share that living with autism can be hard, frustrating, and chaotic but also, at times, brilliant, inspired, and pleasantly unpredictable."

—DR. PAULA KLUTH,
AUTHOR OF "YOU'RE GOING TO LOVE THIS KID":
TEACHING STUDENTS WITH AUTISM IN THE INCLUSIVE CLASSROOM

"To connect with a child with autism is a very special gift . . . not only for the child, but for the few people lucky enough to develop that connection. Robert Parish is sharing this gift with the world."

—JENNIFER STRAUSS, M.ED,
EXECUTIVE PROGRAM DIRECTOR,
AUTISM CONSULTING & TRAINING, INC., MIAMI

"Robert Parish and his contributors provide a perfect blend of first person insights about autism spectrum disorders. Their accounts are informative, uplifting and hopeful, whether you're working with ASD kids in the classroom, or your living room."

—SARAH E. CARUSO,
CARDINAL HILL UNIVERSITY

"An extraordinary collection of stories that allows us to better understand, appreciate, and connect with children on the autism spectrum. These personal accounts provide insight, encouragement, and optimism to families and professionals working with this remarkable and inspiring group of children."

—LINDSEY STERLING, M.S.,
UNIVERSITY OF WASHINGTON AUTISM CENTER

EMBRACING AUTISM

EMBRACING AUTISM

CONNECTING AND

COMMUNICATING

WITH CHILDREN

IN THE AUTISM SPECTRUM

[ROBERT PARISH AND FRIENDS]

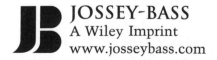

JOSSEY-BASS
A Wiley Imprint
www.josseybass.com

Published by Jossey-Bass
A Wiley Imprint
989 Market Street, San Francisco, CA 94103-1741—www.josseybass.com

Readers should be aware that Internet Web sites offered as citations and/or
sources for further information may have changed or disappeared between the
time this was written and when it is read.

Limit of Liability/Disclaimer of Warranty: While the publisher and author have
used their best efforts in preparing this book, they make no representations
or warranties with respect to the accuracy or completeness of the contents of
this book and specifically disclaim any implied warranties of merchantability
or fitness for a particular purpose. No warranty may be created or extended
by sales representatives or written sales materials. The advice and strategies
contained herein may not be suitable for your situation. You should consult with
a professional where appropriate. Neither the publisher nor author shall be
liable for any loss of profit or any other commercial damages, including but not
limited to special, incidental, consequential, or other damages.

Jossey-Bass books and products are available through most bookstores. To
contact Jossey-Bass directly call our Customer Care Department within the U.S.
at 800-956-7739, outside the U.S. at 317-572-3986, or fax 317-572-4002.

Jossey-Bass also publishes its books in a variety of electronic formats. Some
content that appears in print may not be available in electronic books.

Library of Congress Cataloging-in-Publication Data

    Embracing autism : connecting and communicating with children in the
autism spectrum / Robert Parish and friends.—1st ed.
      p.   cm.
    Includes bibliographical references and index.
    ISBN-13: 978-0-7879-9586-7 (cloth)
      1. Autism in children.   I. Parish, Robert, 1951–
RJ506.A9E445   2008
618.92'85882—dc22

                             2007044099

Printed in the United States of America
FIRST EDITION
HB Printing 10 9 8 7 6 5 4 3 2 1

[CONTENTS]

To Jack Michael Parish,
for always being exactly who you are.

[A C K N O W L E D G M E N T S]

Hundreds of loving, supportive people have been involved in creating this volume about embracing children and adults diagnosed with autism spectrum disorders (ASDs). I will resist the temptation to name them all.

It seems appropriate to first acknowledge my "co-creator" of Jack Michael Parish: his mother, Diane Maier Knight. Despite the fact that Diane and I endured a difficult divorce nearly a decade ago, her vitally important role in Jack's life is recognized and appreciated.

Jack's three older siblings have also made a huge difference in our family's journey with autism. Graham and Ryan Parish (technically, Jack's half-brothers), although not present in his day-to-day life, have—inspired by Jack—embarked on careers working with special children and adults, and they've helped me embrace my youngest son's "difference" more than they'll ever know.

Courtney Parish, at this writing nearly sixteen years old, has been an amazing presence in our family. For a number of reasons, Jack's diagnosis has had a significant impact on nearly every aspect of her life. More often than not, she's handled all the curve balls thrown at her head with humor, understanding, and grace.

Jack's grandparents, Blanche and Jack Maier, have lent important financial support to Jack's therapy and educational life. Sadly, many of the interventions we (and most every other ASD parent) pursue are not covered by insurance.

Arnold Miller and Stephen Shore, who you'll meet on these pages, have been with our family from the beginning of our autism trek. Both have taught me about acceptance and embracing our son for who he actually is.

The editorial and marketing team at Jossey-Bass have been a pleasure to work with. Editor Margie McAneny, who approached me about writing a book during a special education conference in Salt Lake City, has guided this project with passion, professionalism, and humor. Leslie Tilley's content and editorial suggestions shaped the entire manuscript—not an easy task with nearly a dozen writers involved. Other important Jossey-Bass contacts who I've relied on through my maiden "big time" publishing voyage include production editor Matt Hoover, copyeditor Tom Finnegan, senior editorial assistant Julia Parmer, executive editor Lesley Iura, senior marketing manager Dimi Berkner, and publicist Maria Meneses. Thank you all for your creativity and energy.

All the very talented and insightful contributors to this work deserve special mention. For several, it was a first attempt at writing their thoughts and feelings about this mysterious and perplexing difficulty. Everyone, including the already published writers, handled my editorial direction without the slightest bit of hesitation or pride of authorship. Thanks so much for trusting me.

It is important for me to acknowledge a trio of mentors. Sadly, all have passed away. Vivian Kwiatek, my English teacher at Millburn High School in Millburn, New Jersey, was the first one to recognize my "gift" for writing. Courtney Whitney Jr., during my teenage "what should I do for a living?" crisis, gently encouraged me to pursue a career in media and communications. Last but not least is legendary Cincinnati broadcast journalist Al Schottelkotte—absolutely, positively the best writer I've ever worked with.

Finally, a special acknowledgment to my mother, Beverly Jane Acomb Parish, who through example showed me the true meaning of unconditional love. My ability to connect with Jack and write and edit a book about this not-so-comfortable subject is a direct result of her presence in my life.

[ABOUT THE EDITOR]

Robert Parish is an award-winning journalist with four internationally broadcast television documentaries about autism spectrum disorders (ASD) to his credit. Parish has also produced more than one hundred digital video segments about ASD for educational distribution. His projects are used in coursework at universities; by professional associations; and to inspire and educate special education teachers, the medical community, and parents. Parish maintains a Website (www.comebackjack.org) that receives thousands of visitors each month. He is frequently interviewed in the media as an expert on autism. He also hosts a bimonthly program on Autism One Radio. His son Jack has been an inspiration to him, his family, and thousands (perhaps millions) of others.

[ABOUT THE CONTRIBUTORS]

Mother of ten-year-old Jacob, *Diane Bayer* has written extensively for dozens of ASD-oriented Websites, blogs, and electronic publications about her son, his diagnosis, and her perspective about it. She has a master's degree in special education. Her Website is www.theautismexpress.com.

Robert Becerra is an executive in the insurance industry, a budding novelist, and, thanks to his son, Robert Jr. ("Little"), a dedicated student of ASD. He and his wife, Teresa, spend a great deal of time advocating for their own son and countless children and adults with an ASD diagnosis.

Teresa Becerra lives in Miami with her husband, Robert. Her son, Robert Jr., was diagnosed with autism at twenty-three months. She is the founder of I Know Someone with Autism—Now You Do Too, a Dade County School program. She is also the president of Parents for Exceptional Progress, South Florida Chapter. In addition, she lectures at local universities and serves on a number of special education boards. She was recently elected president of the Autism Society of Miami.

Kristina Chew is an assistant professor of classics in the Department of Modern and Classical Languages at Saint Peters College in northern New Jersey. She is also the mom of a young boy with ASD (Charlie) and the publisher of "AutismLand" (www.kristinachew.com), a popular blog.

Gay and Dennis Debbaudt are the proud parents of Brad, a twenty-three-year-old who has autism. They have written reviews of autism-related books for the *Detroit Free Press*. Dennis has written about autism and law enforcement issues for the *FBI Law Enforcement Bulletin, Sheriff* magazine, *The Autism Advocate,* and the Eunice Kennedy Shriver Center at the University of Massachusetts School of Medicine. He has also written a book on this topic for Jessica Kingsley Publishers and created training curriculum and video for law enforcement in North America and Europe. (www.autismriskmanagement.com)

Kristin Kaifas-Tennyson is a graduate of Illinois State University with a degree in education and a concentration in learning disabilities and severe behavior disorders. She has a diverse background in teaching special education, writing behavioral and skill programs for children and adults with mental retardation and other developmental disabilities, and operating group homes and supported living programs for private agencies in the Indianapolis, Cleveland, and Cincinnati areas. She is the principal of an alternative school for children with special needs in Cincinnati.

Jeanne Lyons is the mother of seventeen-year-old Shawn, who has Asperger's Syndrome. Shawn collects and studies exotic plants and has twice been a guest on the *Tonight Show with Jay Leno.* Jeanne writes and performs songs for and about people along the autism spectrum. Her CD, *Gather Stars for Your Children: Songs to Enhance Social Skills and Foster a Welcoming Attitude,* received the Autism Society of America's 1998 Musical Contribution of the Year Award. She has presented autism awareness programs in schools throughout the country. (www.lyonstunes.com)

Jackie Marquette has more than twenty years of experience as a special educator and school consultant. She wrote *Independence Bound,* a book about finding and establishing independent living for her son, Trent. Jackie developed the ACT Project in Kentucky through the Kentucky Autism Training Center, which established employment supports for young adults with ASD. Jackie received her Ph.D. from the University of Louisville, where she studied how youths with ASD reached independent living. Trent has autism, is employed, and has lived independently with "creative supports" for six years. (www.independencebound.com)

Cammie McGovern was awarded a creative writing fellowship at Stanford University and has received numerous prizes for her short fiction. Her stories have appeared in such magazines as *Glamour, Ladies Home Journal, Redbook,* and *Seventeen,* and she is the author of the novel *The Art of Seeing.* She lives in Amherst, Massachusetts, with her husband and three children, the eldest of whom has a diagnosis of autism. She is one of the founders of Whole Children, a resource center that runs after-school classes and programs for children with special needs. Her recent novel *Eye Contact,* a mystery focusing on a young boy with ASD, has been a critical and commercial success. (www.cammiemcgovern.com)

Arnold Miller, director of the Language and Cognitive Development Center of Boston and affiliate professor of psychology, Clark University, received his doctorate in clinical psychology from Clark University. He has held research appointments at Boston University and Harvard Medical School, served on the faculty of the University of Montana, and directed the Language Development Laboratory at Wrentham State School in Massachusetts. He and his late wife, Eileen, founded the internationally respected Language and Cognitive Development Center (LCDC) in Boston in 1965. From then to the present—with the help of research and demonstration grants from the U.S. Department of Education—the Millers have introduced a range of innovative strategies for helping developmentally challenged children achieve their fullest potential. (www.millermethod.org)

Susan Senator is a widely read writer, speaker, political activist, wife, mother of three boys, popular blogger, and belly dancer. The author of *Making Peace with Autism: One Family's Story of Struggle, Discovery, and Unexpected Gifts,* Senator has written dozens of articles and essays on disability, education, parenting, and living happily in publications such as the *Washington Post,* the *New York Times,* the *Boston Globe, Exceptional Parent Magazine, Family Fun,* and *Education Week.* Senator's oldest son, Nat, was diagnosed with autism at the age of three. Her publications, event listings, and blog can be found at www.susansenator.com.

Diagnosed as a youth with "atypical development with strong autistic tendencies," *Stephen Shore* was viewed as "too sick" to be treated on an outpatient basis and recommended for institutionalization. Nonverbal until four, and with much help from his parents, teachers, and others,

Stephen recently completed his doctoral degree in special education. He is also an accomplished author and presenter. He has authored or coauthored three books, including the 2006 Wiley release *Autism for Dummies*. (www.autismasperger.net)

Kim Stagliano has been an autism activist since the oldest of her three autistic daughters was diagnosed in 1996. Never accepting the blunt, dire diagnosis given by the doctors, Kim embarked on a mission to find internal and external treatments that would work best for her children. She contributes to the *Huffington Post*'s Fearless Voices column as "the Autism Mom," and she has written a humorous novel with an autism twist. She runs an autism biomedical support group on Yahoo and serves as a committee member for the National Autism Association. Married to Mark since 1991, she lives in Connecticut with their three girls. Her blog is at www.kimstagliano.blogspot.com.

[FOREWORD]

THE "SECRET" KEY
TO CONNECTION

The big secret to connecting successfully with a child or adult in the autism spectrum is that there is no secret. But that doesn't mean it's easy. Much has already been said, done, and written about autism spectrum disorders (ASDs), especially since 1989 (when my son Nat was born) and 1994 (when he was diagnosed).

Yet the magnitude of literature and accrued wisdom does not make this particular mission any more straightforward. The wealth of conferences, autism experts, therapists, and myriad approaches and therapies all deepen our collective knowledge and understanding of people with ASD, and maybe they give us a flash of inspiration here and there. But what about the actual interacting, educating, connecting, and carrying it out with the right mixture of discipline, compassion, creativity, and, of course, humor? This is something you cannot learn from an expert. However, just as parents learn that their children with the diagnosis are not a mystery, puzzle, or creature, but rather simply a person, so can others learn their own special way of reaching ASD children.

What, then, is the key to dealing with autism? To paraphrase from the location mantra of real estate agents: "acceptance, acceptance, acceptance!" Acceptance, however, is hard for many to come by.

Like so many parents I know, I went through years of wondering and worrying, of not understanding why I could not get little Nat to play with toys other than to line them up or mouth them. Or why he showed no interest in other children but seemed to be content for hours looking at the dust in a sunbeam. And then, after we knew for sure, there were the years of the learning curve, the confusion about what to do for him, how to do it for him, along with my grief over this change in the direction my life was supposed to take.

Once I realized it was really OK that Nat was the way he was, that there was no shame, there was no failure of anything going on, there was nothing that had to change, nothing I had to do except help him learn, I was happier. I was better at parenting him too. I could work with the boy I had, not with some fantasy child created by made-for-TV movies and Hallmark cards. But to do this, I had to trust my gut.

The first breakthrough I had with Nat was with a technique I figured out intuitively. Having no knowledge of social stories or autism approaches, I created my first social storybook for him, the "Nat Book." My instinct told me, and my husband encouraged me, to make a Thanksgiving guidebook for three-year-old Nat so he would have a way of understanding the upcoming holiday. Using cut-up family pictures, Nat could see in the book who was going to be there, what was going to happen, and how the day would end. I even told him that he might be a little scared, but if he stayed calm and remembered that everyone loved him he would have a good time. After reading it over and over, Nat was convinced that he would! He walked right into my aunt's kitchen reciting snippets of the book. Thanksgiving went completely smoothly—the first successful family outing we'd ever experienced.

Not every day is a breakthrough day; most days are not. The point is to use what you know, and then take the leap. If you work with ASD children, the same principle applies. Be prepared and well versed in autism approaches and educational training, but just as important, suspend what you know and just get to know the kid. A certain degree of letting go of your expectations, prejudices, and baggage has to happen.

In letting go of so much, I feel at times as though I am in some ways on my own, which is a scary feeling but also empowering. I am navigating uncharted territory, where I follow my feelings and intuition as well as my autism education, but most important, I follow Nat's cues to gain my insights. When I created the "Nat Book," it was out of sheer desperation, but it was also from the knowledge that books appeared to be the only things outside of himself that interested Nat.

Because ASD children can be unpredictable, intense in what they do, and difficult to read, connection is difficult to come by. Yet I have seen that connection can be difficult with "typical" children too. Or for that matter with husbands, mothers, or friends. These days I apply the perspective I've gleaned from ASD everywhere. To me, everyone is a little in the spectrum. Everyone has their quirks! My son is just more overt in his, more at one with his desires and pleasures. But I want to connect with my son, so I have to do what it takes to get there. I have to tolerate his testing or evasive behaviors, and stay on his side, because my priority is connection, no matter how his neurology looks.

The secret to happy relationships, autism or not, is acceptance—of what you are, and of what he is, warts, synaptic gaps, and all. Then, forging a relationship anyway. It is a bit of an act of faith, at first, an existential journey. But if you literally follow a page from "Nat's Book" ("stay calm") and remain confident that it will happen between you, and that everything really is OK though just different, you will get there. It may not look like anything you've ever known, but this is actually the best part.

The book in your hands is a treasure of epiphanies from those who have been there and who are there. You will find a variety of experiences with the autism spectrum, from people who have lived with ASD in one way or another. Some of the voices—they come from an accomplished professional in the spectrum, nationally recognized educators, a passionate group of autism parents—are wryly witty, while some are raw with emotion; others are in between.

All of the stories offer insights that will both move and educate those working with ASD children, imbuing you the reader with a perspective on ASD that is at once helpful, genuine, and hopeful.

Susan Senator
Brookline, Massachusetts
April 2007

[INTRODUCTION]

By our societal standards, my three oldest children are considered "normal."

My youngest, Jack, is not. His "abnormality" has the unwieldy and undesirable label of autism spectrum disorder (ASD).

Identified by Dr. Leo Kanner at Johns Hopkins University in Baltimore in 1943, ASD has confounded and frustrated an impressive array of the world's foremost medical and educational minds for more than six decades. Theories of its cause have ranged from "cold parenting" to "genetic predisposition" to "oh my God, there's something in the water."

Those of us fortunate enough to have regular contact with ASD children and adults are mostly baffled by the *why* of it as well. The first coherent sentence I wrote about Jack's label many years ago featured the words *mysterious* and *perplexing*.

For me and all the contributors to this book, ASD remains an unsolved mystery. As you'll read, we're beyond trying to solve it; that's up to others. Research in the scientific and educational arenas is heavily funded, meticulous, and perpetual. Breakthroughs happen every day. Undoubtedly, more are on the horizon.

I've often said that one of the most profound things about the ASD journey is the people one meets thanks to the diagnosis. Despite his apparent lack of social networking skills, Jack has introduced me to thousands of thoughtful, articulate, and passionate parents and professionals. In fact, everyone you'll meet on these pages falls into this category.

Of course, we all have a common bond. But part of me feels there is a much larger and more important meaning to our connection. I suppose this book is tangible evidence of that feeling.

The personal perspectives shared here will enhance your reality and resilience, insight and inspiration, and energy and empathy, whether you're linked with ASD in a classroom, on the playground, or in your own backyard.

Some of the stories may break your heart. Others will make you laugh out loud. Some will do both.

Our goal has been, is, and will continue to be determining ways to move beyond curing and coping. This often means wracking our limited neurotypical brains and exploring our own perception of reality to pluck moments of one-on-one connection—to truly be there for this amazing population of human beings.

Thankfully, since Jack's diagnosis in 1996, the public perception of ASD has changed dramatically. Autism is no longer viewed as a terrifying and hopeless diagnosis. As my friend Stephen Shore (Chapter Six), who proudly resides in the spectrum, puts it, "ASD is not a monolithic dragon to be slain."

Children and adults are no longer "afflicted." They're "affected." The spectrum has no beginning, no end, no limitations. To me and many others, ASD is not a disorder. It's a difficulty, or a difference to be worked with.

Don't misunderstand. Connecting with ASD takes patience, persistence, and timing. But when you think about it, anything that matters does. Jack has taught me much about everything. Although our time together can be incredibly frustrating, when we're truly connected the experience is electrifying.

Who's to say the ASD view of the world is impaired? Jack lives every day with more authentic joy than most of us. He never intentionally tries to mess with others' minds or hurt people's feelings (although he manages to do so regularly). Mickey Mouse makes him laugh. Tigger inspires him to jump up and down with squealing delight. The Little Mermaid's songs soothe his sometimes-restless spirit.

He loves crunching (the louder the better) extra crispy, overly salty french fries. Sucking hard through a straw to find every last drop of a chocolate milkshake. Inhaling a thick, greasy hamburger. My son puts ketchup on cheese! He detests brushing his teeth. Haircuts scare the hell out of him. He parties like a naked sailor in the bathtub.

Best of all, Jack loves his mommy, adores his big sister, tolerates his daddy and older brothers, and most important is generally content with being.

Content with being.

There's a concept we can all learn from.

Robert Parish (Jack's dad)
Cincinnati, Ohio
August 2007

EMBRACING AUTISM

1

MY JOURNEY WITH JACOB

[BY DIANE BAYER]

(Diane Bayer, her husband, and two children live in North Carolina.
A former teacher with a master's degree in special education, she has
written extensively about ASD since her son Jacob was diagnosed
in 1999. —RP)

Minnie

The long wooden table divided us. Minnie and Frank sat on one side, and we
professionals sat on the other. Our common bond was the education of their
only son, Sam.

Sam, thirty-five and having profound mental retardation and autism, was nearly blind and partially deaf. He was completely nonverbal and had a penchant for placing his hand up to his throat and making a honking sound. Because he could not communicate his basic needs, Sam was quite a challenge to those of us who worked at the therapeutic day program.

Making matters more interesting, Sam was only partially toilet trained and also possessed a stubborn strength of hunkering down to the floor, "Gumby style," when he didn't feel like moving.

Minnie and Frank, then in their seventies, had been caring for their son with very little help for decades. The family lived together in a small one-bedroom apartment within the city. Pen poised, I began the meeting by discussing possible therapeutic goals for Sam.

My proposed goals were concrete and directly functional, such as teaching Sam how to use sign language to indicate he needed to use the bathroom. I was in midsentence when Minnie interrupted me with her soft southern drawl: "May I say something please?"

Pausing, I put my pen down, and said, "Yes of course. What would you like to tell us?" Frank sat quietly beside his wife, looking down at his hands. Minnie let out a little sigh and began to tell the story that we therapists could not glean from any of our ancient files on Sam's developmental history. It was a story of a mother and father's profound love for their only child. I leaned back in my chair to listen.

Minnie, who was just beginning to experience midlife, and her husband were visiting Germany when she went into labor prematurely. Sam was born with a host of problems, which seemed insurmountable to the attending German medical staff. They predicted that Sam's quality of life would be so negligible that they posted a sign above his crib: "Do Not Feed."

The staff was unaware that Minnie and Frank could read German. Minnie saw the sign and demanded it be taken down at once. She was heartbroken that their son was deemed utterly unworthy of care. But Minnie and Frank did care and did choose to love this child when most everyone else wanted to give up on him.

So Minnie told us that she would never give up hope for the boy who was now a grown man. There was a communal silence on the professional side of the table. Minnie was not quite finished and paused only slightly before asking the question that would tear me up inside. Looking directly at me, she asked, "Could you do one thing for me? Could you please teach him to say 'Mama'?"

I met her eyes and was about to say the truth. The truth was that her Sam would most likely never be able to say a single word, even *Mama*. Yet there was something pure about her request. It spoke to the inseparable bond between mother and child. All these years had passed and she was still waiting, still hoping beyond hope.

Who was I to dash her dreams? I replied, "I'll try."

I can tell you honestly that I never did achieve that goal. Minnie and Frank have long since passed away. She died never having heard her son say "Mama." I still think about that family. After my son Jacob was born, I found myself thinking about them a lot as, almost a decade later, the tables were turned.

On one side sits a diagnostician, an occupational therapist, a speech therapist, a psychologist, and a case manager. My husband and I sit on the other side. We wait for the necessary papers to be shuffled and the meeting to begin. Everything seems so normal, so ordinary, but we know after this meeting our lives will never be ordinary or normal again.

When the professionals deliver the news that our son has autism, it validates everything I have been seeing but refused to believe. Jacob had some of the classic early signs. He used only a few words, he didn't point to things, he refused to engage in direct eye contact, and he didn't come when we called his name.

As much as I already knew about autism, as much as I was educated and trained and had years of clinical experience behind me, I could not process that my son could have autism. I could not emotionally accept the obvious.

After hearing the *A* word announced, I sit stoically at first. But then the questions begin welling up inside of me, all those questions without answers. I ask some of the very same questions posed to me from parents who once sat on the opposite side of the table.

"Will he get better?"

"What will life be like for him? for us?"

"Will he be able to talk?"

I then ask the question that brought me full circle back to Minnie so many years ago.

"Will he ever call me Mommy?"

As the professionals begin to respond, it is as though I'm caught by a wave and forced under water. The rushing in my ears drowns out all sound. I'm unable to hear their muted replies. I know instinctively that they can't see the future. Nobody can.

My only hope is that I find some way to connect with Jacob. Like Minnie, I will love my son even if he never speaks a single word. As a parent, I am humbled by the human need to love and be loved by my child.

Speaking the Language of the Natives

There was a day shortly after my son's diagnosis when I saw a large fountain, the kind where you toss in a coin and make a wish. I looked at Jacob sitting silently in his stroller, entranced by the movement of the water.

With a flick of my wrist, I released both the coin and my wish into the spray. I wished someday to have a conversation with my son. At that time, such a wish seemed a remote possibility.

To have a conversation, the ability to employ words is very useful. Yet when Jacob was diagnosed with autism at the age of three, he had no words at all. In fact, he didn't point, make eye contact, or respond to his name. He didn't seem to possess even the basic preverbal skills necessary to learn language. He babbled incessantly to himself, but it didn't appear that he wanted to or understood how to connect sounds to meaning and intention.

I remember taking him to a toy store, his small frame slumped in the stroller. I would see other children excitedly pointing out toys they wanted to buy. Not Jacob. He didn't seem to want anything. If he had shown any sign of desire, I would have been prepared to buy any toy in that store. He just needed to give me a sign. The sign did not come. More often than not on such visits, we would go home empty-handed.

We had several sad Christmas mornings where I would place a present before him and Jacob would either look blindly at the package or walk away. I felt as though he were a tourist in our world.

How could I share my world with him if we didn't have any way to communicate with each other?

Early on, I understood that if I were to have any hope of connecting with my son I would need to stop assuming that he would have all the same wants and needs of a typical child. I would begin to play detective, observing when he did show desire. I observed that Jacob played with traditional toys, but quite often other objects would hold more of his fascination—as with our broom. It was through Jacob's attachment to this broom that we were able to experience one of our very first connections.

Jacob would reach for the broom, not for the purpose of sweeping but to get lost in the pattern of its strands. He was enraptured by how each yellow strand fell into place as he flicked his fingers repetitively though them. He was so spellbound by his broom play that he would choose it over anything, including toys or even food. Now that I had found the object of his desire, I would use this attachment as a basis for connection. I placed his beloved broom up on a high shelf, one that he could not possibly reach. Jacob pushed my hands up toward the broom to get it. When that did not work, he tried to climb up my body to reach it. I told him that if he really wanted the broom he would have to make some sort of sound for it.

I had him watch my mouth as I repeated the word *broom*. I had no idea whether this strategy would work or not, but I kept trying. Jacob was rapidly becoming frustrated, not seeming to understand what I was wanting from him. Growing weary myself, I almost abandoned my efforts.

And then I heard it. It was like a ghost word, so delicate and airy it had almost gone through my consciousness unnoticed. He made the best approximation of the word he was able to do: "booohm." I swooped up his body and scared him with my joy. I gave him the broom and he began to caress the golden strands like hair.

This was the just the beginning of Jacob's language development. Along with *booohm,* he would add the word *go* to his verbal repertoire. This erupted in the middle of the night. Jacob stood up in his crib and was attempting to climb over the rails when he wailed, "Go!" It was loud, it was clear, and there was no misunderstanding of what he meant. Other words followed: *more, milk, up.* Each time he would say a particular word, I wrote it down, hoping for the day when my list exceeded fifty words.

Part of this initial list were number words and the alphabet. Jacob learned to recite the alphabet and count far sooner than he learned names for people. I waited patiently a couple more years before I heard him call for me by name.

My wish seemed to be coming true as Jacob's list of words grew to several pages. I stopped counting after a couple hundred words. Early on, I had wondered if Jacob would ever be able to talk at all. Then I wondered what he might say to me once he did learn language. I found he would use language in highly unusual ways. As much as he was learning my language, I was also learning his.

Here are some examples of Jacobspeak, followed by translation:

- "Elephant!" means "I'm extremely angry right now!"

- "Circus Clown," often spoken in a sneering tone. Jacob is telling someone that she's an idiot.

- "Holiday!" Jacob's way of granting himself immunity from doing something he doesn't wish to do: "Don't bother me with your silly requests; I'm declaring a holiday."

- "Frog, frog, frog" is a chant he developed to calm himself down when upset. Quite often, he jumps to the words.

- "Birthday party! Toot! Toot!" is his way of telling us whatever is going on is not making him happy as a birthday party would.

- "Little Blue Engine please help us," is cried out when he's frustrated and in need of help.

I find that I must assume the role of interpreter as he makes those forays into reaching out through words. Connection does not come easily for Jacob; he doesn't fully speak the language of the natives.

True connection is a reciprocal process. We can never assume our world is the only world. I had to put one foot into Jacob's world as much as he must step forth into mine. He learned but one way to merge both worlds through spoken language. Could we discover other ways to connect as mother and son?

All in a Song

There is one phrase every mother wants to hear from her child. It's the fundamental message from which primary bonds are formed: "I love you."

I had spoken these words out loud and in soft whispers to Jacob from the first moments I could hold him. After he was diagnosed, I anticipated that

I might never hear those words said back to me—a logical assumption to make for a child who had so little use for words.

When I finally did hear my son say "I love you," the words were sung and not spoken.

When we first began making forays to connect with Jacob, it was suggested that we try music as a means to connect. It seemed an obvious choice. He had always shown a passion for music. Even as an infant, we would catch him holding onto the sides of his crib, wriggling to the rhythms of a song played on the radio. Later, he would demand certain songs be played over and over from videos or tapes. He would try to sing his favorite songs, only to have them come out garbled from running all the sounds together in a never-ending cacophonous stream.

We helped Jacob comprehend the lyrics he heard by purposefully slowing down the songs we sang to him, carefully pausing between words. We also paired written song lyrics with visual icons, creating a rebus of sorts. We enjoyed success when we heard him sing songs with more precision and clarity than he could muster using spoken language alone. Music was quickly becoming a marvelous conduit for communication and connection.

There was another strategy we employed to get him to participate in a musical reciprocity of give-and-take. We would sing a verse and pause, waiting for him to finish singing the rest of the words. This was the very strategy I used to conjure the phrase I had been longing to hear.

I sang the words to a familiar song—"You are my sunshine, my only sunshine. You make me happy when skies are gray. You'll never know dear how much . . . "—and paused at that exact moment to wait for his soft little voice to follow with "I love you." There was no way around the fact that I had used trickery to fill my emotional needs; I was only slightly ashamed. It felt good to hear those words from Jacob for the very first time, whether it was an illusion or not.

I wondered, though, if Jacob truly understood the words he was hearing and singing. Did they have any internal meaning for him? I would find as time went on that he did, in fact, understand more of the depth and feeling to songs than I could ever imagine. When he could not articulate what he wanted to say in words, he would tell me in a song.

There was a day when Jacob was terribly angry with me. It was raining and we could not go to his favorite park. He did not or would not understand the very real parameters posed by uncontrollable weather. He began to have a tantrum, yelling and thrashing limbs, and then suddenly he bounded up to his room and shut the door.

I stood outside his bedroom and was about to enter when I heard an unmistakable bellow of rage coming from his tape player: "You're a Mean One, Mr. Grinch!" The words of his message came straining at full volume from the crack of his doorway: "Your heart's an empty hole. Your brain is full of spiders. You've got garlic in your soul."

It was an effective way for Jacob to tell me off without actually doing so directly. Indirect or not, it was clear to me that I was a female version of the Grinch!

There were many more instances of Jacob using music to convey his mood and message to us and to the world. He has a love for Disney music; consequently, we own most of the Disney song collection. From this rather large selection, he has but a few songs that he plays repetitively. At first, I thought his choices were random; as I listened to the words to these songs I knew he chose to play them for a reason.

Jacob wants to be heard.

There are days when he uses his room as a refuge, looking out his window and playing his music. One song he chooses to play during these reflective times is from the Disney *Tarzan* movie, entitled "Strangers Like Me" and sung by Phil Collins:

Whatever you do, I'll do it too
Show me everything and tell me how
It all means something
And yet nothing to me

I can see there's so much to learn
It's all so close and yet so far
I see myself as people see me
Oh, I just know there's something bigger out there

I wanna know, can you show me
I wanna know about these
strangers like me
Tell me more, please show me
Something's familiar about these strangers like me

When I first saw these lyrics in print, I nearly cried. The words clearly convey the challenges of everyday life for my son. He knows he is different. He has come to realize that he is sometimes a stranger in our world. With this knowledge comes pain and frustration. But as the song says, "Oh, I just know there's something bigger out there." The something bigger is love and connection.

This need for connection grew as Jacob developed and matured. Spoken language and music were only the beginning to his attempts to share himself with me and the world. We also discovered one of his strongest talents from within the realm of our unique relationship as mother and son.

Autism and Artism

In my bedroom closet, there's a box filled with drawing papers of all colors and sizes. Some are wrinkled and torn near the edges. They are all remarkable in their own right, yet one stands out from the rest. It is a bright fluorescent green sheet of paper decorated with four circles arranged within a sphere. A fifth circle spins in its own orbit alongside the rest. These seemingly random shapes scrawled with black crayon would seem insignificant to anyone not understanding their history.

My son's passion and talent for art began with a simple circle. It also marked the creation of yet another pathway toward communication and connection.

Prior to his diagnosis, Jacob showed no ability or desire to draw. During the testing process, he was asked to draw a circle following the therapist's model. Not only did he ignore her instructions, he bounded up from his chair and began to play with the window blinds. He had found rapture in the rhythmic up-and-down pull of the cord and saw no need for circle drawing.

I remember going home dismayed. His failure to imitate this simple task did not bode well for his cognitive development.

When we got home, I kept replaying the scene from the testing room in my mind. Jacob had failed to respond, but did that necessarily mean he was incapable of doing what he had been asked? There was a part of me desperate to see him draw the circle. I believed my son to be much more capable than the diagnostic tests allowed, but how was I to discover the truth?

I began to read accounts from other parents about the experience of raising a child with autism. In my reading, I found one particular story quite compelling. A mother described how her daughter would hide her skills and talents. This seemed all too familiar. When Jacob turned two, he began to recite the entire alphabet, seemingly out of the blue. I caught him saying it to himself while facing the door to his closet. I had no idea he had been learning and practicing, because I had never heard him say a single letter out loud. This skill seemed to emerge out of nothingness. He was learning, even if I was not there to witness it. When he finally did share his ability, he did so by burrowing his face into my lap so I could not see him. Only then, when he was assured that I could not look at him directly, did he recite the alphabet in my presence.

I kept reading. This mother had found a way to discover her daughter's true capabilities without triggering her child's anxiety of exposure. She would present her daughter with a task and then leave, allowing her child to work alone. It was when her daughter knew she was not being watched or observed that she would demonstrate her knowledge and skills. My mind began exploring the possibilities of seeing if this might hold true for Jacob as well. I would wait until morning, and we would try the circle test again.

I drew four circles on a sheet of paper and showed my efforts to Jacob. I felt myself stiffen, preparing for disappointment. I gave the paper to him while he was sitting in a big easy chair, his small legs dangling over the seat cushion. I placed the pencil beside him and gave him directions to draw another circle. I left him, closed my eyes, and waited for several minutes. It was all I could stand.

I came back and he was still sitting there staring and making babbling sounds as though nothing had happened. My heart sank until I looked. There it was! My hope! That fifth circle was there! I just about cried. I hugged his resisting body. I am sure he was unaware of the meaning of his small but magnificent gesture.

He could draw the damn circle.

What Jacob would then draw after those glorious moments of discovery was more than astounding. He instinctively understood perspective from the beginning. Houses, igloos, and churches were all equally drawn with depth and precision. Images would flow onto the paper effortlessly and seemingly with no planning or speculation. At first, his artistic fascination consisted of inanimate objects such as buildings and trains. Later he began to draw people and animals, depicting them from his unique perspective. His caricatures are full of personality and express a range of human emotions. I see my son in these drawings, his passion pouring out of a black stub of a crayon. With the same flourish of his small hands he is able to draw a powerful locomotive or show awareness of the social intricacies of a birthday party.

Even more profound than Jacob's amazing technical abilities is his use of drawing as a way to communicate and connect. What he is unable to express through words, he is able to draw. We have discovered together that we do not need words to have a conversation. On the day he wanted to go strawberry picking, for example, he did not need words to convey his wishes. He drew them instead. He carefully laid a series of pictures on the kitchen floor. A drawing of a strawberry, a church seen within view of the strawberry field, and a basket clearly told the story of his desire. In comparison, words would not have given me such a rich portrait of Jacob's world. A beautiful world it is, complete with giant pocked strawberries and the majestic pillars of a beloved church.

Other such wordless conversations followed. We found that we could even have an argument through his art. Jacob was having an emotional meltdown one day and crying at the top of his lungs. When I tried to intervene, I found myself growing angry; my voice rose in volume to compete with his wailing. He then took a sheet of paper and began sketching angrily. A woman's face appeared with a huge open mouth. The next thing I knew, garbage was being drawn coming out of the mouth. I drew another picture back at him, of a little boy who was yelling. Jacob stopped crying long enough to look at my drawing and then drew a big red line across the image of the mouth spewing garbage. I followed suit and drew a line through my picture of the boy crying. Soon after, I began to laugh at the humor of the situation. We were connecting despite my son's inability to express his anger through words.

Perhaps our methods of communication are not conventional, but we are certainly like any other mother and son in that we sometimes get angry with each other and feel the need to express it.

Along with anger, my son is also able to communicate the fundamental emotion that bonds every parent and child. He is able to show love through artistic expression. I recall a bad morning, when he had cut holes in the tips of his socks and squeezed a tube of toothpaste over several of his stuffed animals. We were upset with each other. I did not understand his behavior that day, and he did not understand my rules. In the aftermath, he came to me as I was writing, with his head bowed. In his hands he held a cutout of two joined hearts colored with red magic marker. His hand drew near to mine and he quietly pushed the joined hearts within my grasp. It was the best "I love you" I had ever received. No words were necessary.

The discovery of my son's passion for art was and is nothing short of a miracle. His talent allows us the means to bridge those gaps caused by his disability. A simple circle is the perfect symbol for the dynamic of our connection. He drew a circle and let me in.

Penguin Kisses

What is it like to parent and love a child with autism? In many ways, it is like trying to relate to the cute little extraterrestrial in the movie *ET.* Is it possible? Absolutely. But you have to give up many preconceived notions of what it means to connect. You have to lift your feet off the ground and be willing to fly into the unknown.

There are times when I feel my son is like an alien in our world; he doesn't fully speak the language and has no use for our rules. Our days often include tears of frustration from him trying to adapt to this strange world.

I am his mother, but I am also his teacher and guide. Part of this awesome responsibility is not just to lead but to follow. In following his lead,

I have discovered that love doesn't always come in the form we expect. Much like my son, love refuses to abide by rules of convention.

The stuffed penguin was waiting in the children's section of our local bookstore. When I saw it, I felt an immediate spark. While holding its soft body to my cheek, I immediately knew that I had to take him home to my son.

As I stood in line to make the purchase, I felt a twinge of anxiety. Jacob had not been doing so well behaviorally and seemed to reject every gesture toward connection. The more I reached out to him, the more he pushed me away. I would try to hug his little body only to have him stiffen and run away or yell, "Walk away please!" I would bring him home surprises from my rare solo trips out into the community, only to have him toss them aside with indifference. I was hoping that this little stuffed penguin would somehow make a difference. I wanted my son to accept my gift to him. I wanted him to accept me.

When I got home, Jacob was sitting near the front door, as though he had been waiting for my return. I cautiously brought the penguin out from behind my back and into his view. I braced myself for a rejection, but magic happened. My son took one glance at my penguin offering, and a tiny smile formed on his elfish face. He extended his hands to hold the toy. I was thrilled. An instant bond was formed as though he had found a long-lost friend. But something even more magical then happened.

Although Jacob is not so accepting of hugs and kisses from me directly, he wanted them from this stuffed penguin. He offered the penguin to me and said, "Penguin kiss?" I then proceeded to smother him with kisses from the penguin's plush beak. Interspersed with the penguin kisses, I sneaked in a few of my own, and he accepted them. More requests would come: "Penguin hug?" Never having asked for affection directly from anyone, it was a breakthrough for him to ask for it by way of the fuzzy touch of our penguin friend. Perhaps it feels safer for my son to accept love through a stuffed animal conduit. Whatever the reason, I feel grateful.

We have come full circle. I thought of Minnie today and her unfulfilled wish to have her son call her "Mama." I thought of my own wishes to hear Jacob talk. Not only can he speak; he can sing and draw his thoughts as well.

I thought about my wish at the fountain, to have a conversation with him. Perhaps we do not communicate typically, but somehow we manage to say what needs to be said.

As I was writing this last section, Jacob apparently read my thoughts and paid me a visit. "Beep, beep, beep," he squeaked while pecking my cheek with his penguin.

"Beep, beep, beep," I replied.

It wasn't a traditional "I love you," but it was definitely close enough.

2

RELATING TO
ASD CHILDREN

[BY ARNOLD MILLER]

(Internationally recognized as one of the preeminent experts in autism spectrum disorders, Arnold Miller has been successfully working with ASD children and adults for nearly fifty years. He is the director of Boston's Language and Cognitive Development Center and an affiliate professor of psychology at Clark University. —RP)

"You knock but nobody answers."
"If I'm in his way, he walks over me as if I'm a piece of furniture."
"When he does look at me, he seems to look right through me, as if I'm transparent."

—Parents of ASD children

Children in the autism spectrum are often intimidating to both the parents who live with them and the professionals who are trying to help them.

Faced with the range of behavior the children present, professionals often ask themselves, "Where do I start?" Complicating things further, though one may find him or her very appealing, even beautiful, the child often behaves as if one does not exist.

The felt need is to elicit some kind of response—a fleeting glance, a smile—anything that communicates one is more than wallpaper to the child. But the child does not permit it. "You knock, but nobody answers."

A common second reaction to these children is to rationalize the disorder. It is painful to confront aberrant functioning in a child; one wants to make it go away. As a result, many professionals and parents rationalize the child's difficulty in enacting change or following directions as simply "being stubborn," and resistance to including others in their play as being due to the child's "independent" nature.

Sometimes, pediatricians answer questions from anxious parents about their child's failure to communicate by saying not to worry: "After all, Einstein didn't speak until he was four."

At the more severe end of the autism continuum, the children echo commercials from radio and television, flap their arms and twiddle fingers in front of their face, run in circles or from wall to wall in a room, flick the lights on and off, flush the toilet, line things up, and get lost finding their way to the bathroom. Often too, they demonstrate poor reactivity to pain, are clumsy, and have an uncertain sense of their body.

At the Language and Cognitive Development Center, we have dealt with the challenges of ASD for more than four decades. We found that, to be effective, it is essential that we see the children as they are—not as we would like them to be. Crediting children with more capacity than they have is a serious error because it results in beginning a treatment program that is beyond their reach, with consequent waste of precious time.

The challenge is to help the special child come alive or break through so that when one knocks, someone answers. But what does *break through* mean?

It means that the child responds to a parent and familiar professionals with a smile and delight when one plays with him or her. He or she acknowledges one's existence and returns affection. The child shows through behavior a preference for parent or caregiver over strangers and can play with (and even tease) one. All these behaviors show that he or she is becoming more conscious of the self in relation to others. In short, the child is becoming alive as a person capable of independent action and choices.

The important issue is how best to help the child reach that point. Before discussing what kind of attitude is most helpful, I would like to dispel certain unhelpful notions about the source of the child's disordered behavior. The most important of these notions is the tendency to assume that the child is rejecting or not responding because of poor nurturing or handling, or from willfulness.

The Child's "Difference" Is Not the Fault of Parents

It is completely understandable that one might take a child's unresponsiveness as a rejection. It is important to get past this notion as soon as possible, for two very important reasons.

First, the child's aberrant, nonresponsive behavior is not a rejection of parents or caregivers. The child tends to behave like this with everybody. The distressing behavior of self-preoccupation, eye avoidance, and failure to respond to affection are part of the child's bioneurologically based problem.

The same is true if he or she is a scattered child. By *scattered* we mean children so driven by stimuli in their surroundings—the scraping of chairs, clattering of blocks, movement of the teacher—that they are unable to focus their attention in a productive way to complete tasks.

The child's central nervous system does not allow him or her to take in and process information the way "typical" children do. In other words, the child often does not have the tools to respond to a parent or professional without assistance.

Second, if the child is viewed as rejecting, then a natural and self-protective tendency is to pull back. This can trigger more distressing behavior. The ASD child needs parents and professionals to be emotionally available to reach out and make emotional contact with them.

There Is Often a Bond, Even When It Is Not Immediately Apparent

Parents and professionals need to know that even though a child might not be able to demonstrate feelings in the usual way, this does not mean those feelings are not there. The bond often shows up indirectly when a new baby comes along, or when the teacher becomes involved with another child.

Many times, we have received reports that after a new baby was born and the mother became preoccupied with nursing and caring for it, the ASD child suddenly became very distressed, aggressive, or self-abusive. One mother reported that after the birth she couldn't even go to the bathroom or answer the phone without her special child becoming upset and often developing a major tantrum.

Another mother, driving a car with her special four-year-old child in the seat next to her (and her new infant in a car seat in the rear), turned to attend to the infant and was suddenly attacked by her special child "for no apparent reason."

Sometimes, however, there is not even this indirect expression of a bond. For example, one father reported that when he came home from work his daughter leaped into his arms while his three-year-old son kept turning little animals in his hands and behaving as if the father weren't there, leading this father to report with distress that he "had absolutely no relationship" with his son.

Can a Bond Be Built When There Is None Initially?

Can a bond be created between parent and child, or between professional and child, where there was none initially? The answer, based on our work with thousands of ASD children in our center, is that it can. Even among children who show no apparent relationship with a parent or teacher, we have found that with help many can learn to establish such a positive relationship.

Certain ways of being or styles that parents and professionals have with ASD children work for and against forming a bond; in fact, they contribute strongly to the child's development.

Four Common "Support and Demand" Stances Toward Special Children

There are many ways to establish mutually satisfying contact between a parent or professional and an ASD child. All of these strategies, however, build on an underlying stance. The stance requires that neither parent or professional be overly respectful of the child's neurologically driven tendency toward isolation, self-preoccupation, extreme passivity, or scattered behavior.

I recommend a very active, supportive, but carefully intrusive stance toward the special children with whom we work. I refer to this as a "high support, high demand" stance, which we teach our staff and the parents with whom we work.

Over the years, we have found that those who achieve this stance are most successful in helping children reach their full potential. Stances that work against the emotional and developmental breakthrough we seek are "high support, low demand," "high demand, low support," and "low support, low demand."

As I briefly describe these stances, you may recognize yourself in some of them. Awareness of one's own stance is an important part of working with special children.

HIGH SUPPORT, LOW DEMAND

A parent or professional who carries a child capable of walking, who dresses a child "because it's quicker," and who would much rather keep a five-year-old in the grocery cart than risk having the child push the cart is expressing a high-support, low-demand stance. When we are assessing such a child, a parent often darts in and does for the child what we are trying to assess.

The underlying feeling that drives a mother to behave in this way can be paraphrased: "My child is handicapped . . . injured in some way. Those who would make demands of him are likely to add to his injury (or make his limitations too painfully evident to me). My task as his mother is to protect my injured child (and myself) by helping him avoid demands and by keeping him close to me."

Among professionals, this stance shows itself in oversupporting the child by doing too much hand-over-hand, so that there is little opportunity to determine what the child can do on his or her own.

HIGH DEMAND, LOW SUPPORT

The opposite stance, often adopted by fathers who cannot tolerate the thought of their child being disordered, might be phrased, "There's not a damn thing wrong with my son. . . . I'll see to it that he does everything the other kids do!"

The regime such fathers impose often does not take into account the child's needs. It results in well-meaning but unfortunate bullying of the child to try to do things that are often beyond reach. This stance may induce the child to withdraw further.

Among professionals, this stance is evident in tough teachers who insist on imposing a curriculum on children independent of its relevance to them, and despite it clearly not getting through to the children. Such a teacher might insist on going through the days of the week or the seasons of the year even though the child is unable to anticipate what is going to happen during the next five minutes.

LOW DEMAND, LOW SUPPORT

The saddest stance is one in which one or both parents, depressed or overwhelmed by the demands placed on them by the apparently intractable behavior of their child, have pretty much given up. Their attitude can be paraphrased as "There is nothing you can do with that child . . . so I just let him sit in front of the TV. . . . If he gets too wild I leave him in his room."

Among professionals, this used to express itself in a "don't make waves" attitude: "The kid is not making any trouble by himself, so I just leave him alone." Fortunately, since we began this work, the attitude has become less and less prevalent in classrooms.

In sharp contrast, the high-support, high-demand stance we recommend avoids the errors of overprotectiveness, bullying, or laissez-faire inherent in the other stances. It implies a vigorous, supportive, playful, carefully intrusive, somewhat challenging attitude that shows itself in intolerance of the child "disappearing."

Such withdrawal can be combated by getting in the child's face, by cautiously aggravating him in a variety of ways: putting his shirt half on so he has to struggle to find where his arms go, putting one sock on and "forgetting" to put the other on, forgetting to give him the spoon he needs to eat his soup, getting in his way or "accidentally" bumping into him as he tries to walk past (or over) you, and so forth.

This attitude, in our experience, if employed in concert with appropriate interventions, is the one most likely to lead to substantial gains in all areas.

3

THREE SPECIAL KIDS—NO APOLOGIES NECESSARY

[BY KIM STAGLIANO]

(An ASD activist and published writer, Kim Stagliano has been blessed with three beautiful girls diagnosed with autism. We connected, thanks to our mutual friend and contributor of the Foreword to this volume, Susan Senator. —RP)

I'm not sure I'll ever grow accustomed to the wide-eyed stares I receive from people when I tell them my husband, Mark, and I are the parents of three children diagnosed with autism. I can see the words forming: "Excuse me? You're what?"

"Yes," I confirm with a sheepish smile intended to defuse their discomfort. "Not one, not two, but three kids. We call them our 'autism hat trick.'"

I imagine the questions racing through their mind. How could two healthy adults have three children with autism? (I have my suspicions but rarely discuss them with new acquaintances.) Just what kind of drugs did you do in college, Kim? (I plead the Fifth.) How do you do it? (That one's easy to answer: How could I not? They are my kids!)

What's more extraordinary is that all my children are girls. Autism typically strikes boys four-to-one over girls. We're full of surprises, as is life with children who have an autism spectrum diagnosis.

The Centers for Disease Control and Prevention report that one in 150 American children is being diagnosed as somewhere on the autism spectrum. That's a lot of parents hearing life-altering words from a doctor: "Your child has autism."

A chill always races down my spine when I remember the dreary November day we were told for certain our first two beautiful daughters had autism. The simple words hit me like a one-two punch in the gut.

I had prepared for my pregnancies like an Olympic athlete in training. I taught step aerobics; I ran to keep my weight in check and my muscles strong for the rigors of delivery. I dutifully downed the giant prenatal vitamins my obstetrician prescribed. Liquor did not pass my lips. I ate healthy food, gave up my coffee and sweets. To seal the deal I crafted with God—the one promising me healthy kids—I opted for natural childbirth to ensure the babies were also drug-free. Three deliveries, and not so much as a Tylenol in my system to ease the pain.

Our beautiful Mia Noel was born in December 1994. She was a gorgeous baby. Her large blue eyes followed me; her pink lips formed a perfect circle when she cried for food. She took to the breast easily and gained weight and length right on target. She loved being held as much as I loved cradling her in my arms. She smiled at me every day. I have the photos to prove it. She met her early milestones right on track, rolling over, sitting up, and pulling herself up to standing. Mia spoke her first word at ten months ("shoe").

After one year, the development that had raced forward into what we were certain was sheer brilliance began to slow to a crawl. I began to worry.

I'm grateful that Mark and I were able to savor the sweetness of being first-time parents during those all-too-brief months when we unaware of the freight train bearing down on us. There's nothing to describe the onslaught of love you feel for the child you bring into the world. Or the heartache when you learn there's something "not right."

At two, Mia could read and recite her alphabet and count to twenty. But her vocabulary got stuck at single words and didn't develop into sentences. She knew the word "mom," but she never called out to me. She used the word merely as a label for the woman who fed, bathed, and loved her. "Cup." "Ball." "Mom." When Gianna was born, Mia would not look at her. She had no desire to play mommy, preferring to read and reread her Dr. Seuss ABC book.

I tried to set aside the doubts niggling in the back of my mind, telling myself Mia was too busy reading to pay heed to a new baby. The chasm in my stomach told me otherwise. I spent hours comparing her development to every timeline in *What to Expect the Toddler Years*. I sat, pen in hand, trying to fill in her baby book but having nothing to add. My heart broke looking at those blank pages, so I simply closed the book.

When I was pregnant with our second child, our pediatrician told us Mia had a developmental delay, so we enrolled her in early intervention (EI) services, where she received speech therapy in a preschool setting. I sat at the EI meetings, tears streaming down my face, thankful that someone was rallying to help us. I pretended to have a handle on her problem and devoted my attention to preparing for our new baby, letting the professionals take care of Mia's situation.

Gianna Marie arrived in a breeze of a delivery on July 11, 1996. She was a pretty, fair-haired infant with almond-shaped eyes, green like her dad's. "Lucky 7/11!" we joked of her birth date. Gianna was nothing like her sister as a newborn. Where Mia had been content and easygoing, Gianna was irritable. She was a fussy nurser who bit me to bleeding for months. And she was really loud.

She was a late walker and didn't take her first steps until sixteen months. By two, she wasn't speaking more than a handful of words. She was headstrong and prone to major tantrums. We assumed she was just a different personality from her sister.

Our pediatrician suggested EI services again but assured us he had never heard of a family with more than one child with autism. It was the first time he'd uttered the *A* word to me. I admit, it was a word I'd been trying on for months. I felt the pain and cast aside the thought, reminding myself the doctor told me Mia had only a developmental delay. Surely Gianna was following suit. I clung to his words like a life preserver: "I've never heard of a family with more than one child with autism."

Well, how do you do, doctor? We're the Staglianos.

We received our formal autism diagnoses in 1999 from a neurologist at a highly regarded hospital in the Midwest. We sat in a stark waiting room for more than ninety minutes. The girls got antsy, and Mark and I were scared to death. I filled out a check-off-the-boxes style questionnaire, knowing full well that each *X* scratched onto the pages might mark my girls forever.

The doctor gave the girls a cursory medical exam. Then she asked us lots of questions about play habits, motor skills, milestones, and social interaction. She watched them walk down the hallway, scribbling copious notes on the girls' charts. I knew where my answers and her notes were leading.

Sure enough, at the end of the exam she pronounced that our girls were "autistic." Then she handed me a folder full of the most depressing articles I had ever read and sent us on our way. This brilliant doctor just told us we had two kids with an autism spectrum diagnosis, yet she gave us no plan for their care, no road map to their recovery, and—worse—absolutely no hope.

The first page in that flimsy blue folder had a headline that read, "There is no cure for autism. You can only hope to make an autistic person's life more comfortable." My initial thought was, "Oh really? Well, we'll just see about that." The gravity of having two ASD toddlers started to sink in as we walked out the door. It hurt far more than labor and delivery.

I became pregnant with our third child just two months after Mia and Gianna were diagnosed. I told myself there was no way I could have a third child with the diagnosis. I was wrong. I had the amniocentesis procedure required of a thirty-six-year-old woman, and the results were normal. This pregnancy was not as easy as the first two; I chalked it up to being older and under the stress of caring for two demanding girls aged four and five.

Toward the end of my term, the baby remained stubbornly upside down. Baby Stagliano was breech. I turned down a Cesarean section for two reasons. First, I didn't want the drugs required for the surgery to get into my baby's system. I'm a stubborn woman. I had natural childbirth for my first two children and was determined to do the same for my third. Second, I lived six hundred miles from my mom, had a husband who traveled often for business, and couldn't see how I'd care for a newborn and two challenging sisters after surgery.

My obstetrician offered to flip the baby in utero, a process called a breech version. I agreed. It took three attempts to wrestle the baby 180 degrees around. The process was as painful as labor. But it was pain with a purpose, so I breathed my way through it for the sake of my infant.

Isabella Michelle, a gorgeous Mia look-alike, was born on September 14, 2000. By twelve months, we knew she was yet another incarnation of autism. Bella was a quiet baby who never developed any speech. At age six, she finally began to find her voice and use single-word approximations that only her therapists and I could interpret. I attributed these successes to better schooling that offered abundant therapy, intensive biomedical interventions with a knowledgeable doctor, and a lot of prayers.

I often find myself in the awkward position of having to explain my kids' ASD diagnoses in public. It catches strangers by surprise. Fellow supermarket shoppers might think my girls are rude—or worse, stupid—when they don't respond to a smile or a question. They are neither, I assure you. My girls are smart, and they understand everything that is said to them.

I hate having to sum up my beautiful girls in one word. *Autism* says so much yet tells so little. I wish I could tell them about the joy and happiness the girls bring us. There isn't enough time in the checkout line to explain. Instead I whisper, "She doesn't speak yet. She has autism," to the grocery clerk who offers Bella a lollipop and gets only a blank look. I wear an autism ribbon pin in church to ward off the stares when Mia is reciting Elmo's World dialogue during the Lord's Prayer. Her deep voice interrupts the mass ("Elmo loves you!"). I nod and smile to fellow parishioners to deflect their eyes from Mia.

Mark and I experience the same pride as other parents. We just use a different measuring stick. This gives us a lot of opportunities to cheer. We celebrate the tiniest achievements and revel in every success, no matter how small. For instance, I called my mom to tell her Bella handed me a tiny card that reads, "I'm hungry." I pumped my fist with a silent "yes!" when Gianna navigated a birthday party with ten typical school chums, bestowing on me a peek at her independence. When Mia says, "Hi, Mom," after school, I beam with delight. Each day brings a gift.

It's disconcerting for family, friends, and strangers to see three sisters with autism. But Mark and I wouldn't trade our girls for the world. That's not to say we're content with their autism diagnosis. Loving our kids does not mean we love their autism. This is a controversial statement these days.

There are ASD adults and parents of ASD kids who feel that autism is just another way of being. I respectfully disagree. I like to say that autism is like a box of Bertie Bott's Every Flavor Beans, a candy from the Harry Potter books that comes in flavors ranging from chocolate to charcoal. You can guess which flavor my girls got.

My girls need constant care. Though I'm happy to be there for them for the rest of my days, I'd be lying if I didn't admit that I want my girls to enjoy all the richness of life, including leaving the nest. How could I not want to make their lives easier?

I count my blessings for the magical glimpses of emerging skills we see every day. These flashes are salve for the major heartaches we face when we allow ourselves to think about them. The future is indeed frightening. How will we care for three adults with autism? Where will the money come from? Then there's the question I can barely form on my lips: Will the world care for them when we're gone?

If my girls had asthma, diabetes, or (heaven forbid) cancer, I would leave no stone unturned to care for them. It simply has never occurred to me that autism should be any different. Unfortunately, there is no universally accepted standard of care for kids on the spectrum. A child's chance for improvement depends on what state she lives in, what group of people she connects with, her school district, and the attitude of the presiding doctors. With all these variables, a child's future is left to chance. There's no Ronald McDonald House for autism. No Sloan Kettering or M. D. Anderson Cancer Center. Exhausted parents have to pick and choose their options à la carte.

I know that some children are losing their ASD diagnosis thanks to parents, doctors, and therapists who refuse to write them off or give up on them. Other parents work just as hard and don't see their kids make the same gains.

There's no magic formula at home or in the classroom. I don't know how far along the path to recovery each of my three girls will travel. Perhaps Gianna can get to the point where she just looks like a quirky adult. Maybe Bella will speak well enough to tell people she is hungry, is hurt, or needs a hug. Possibly Mia will be able to order a sandwich for herself at the sub shop.

I just want my girls to be able to look after themselves. That is not even close to saying I want to change them because I am dissatisfied with who they are. I've seen how their autism can handicap them, compromise their safety, and cause them great pain.

When Bella was five, we moved into a new house. Our furniture had been in storage for ten months. The girls were really excited to see their beds, their familiar belongings, and their toys. Bella was playing "monkey on the bed," jumping to her heart's content. I ran into her room to grab her just as she went sailing off the bed, conking her head on the floor.

"Bella! Are you OK?" I asked. I checked her eyes and felt her head. She seemed fine. She wasn't bleeding. Of course she was crying. I assumed she'd scared herself almost as much as she had scared me, and that she was exhausted from a day of moving. I tucked her into bed. Ten minutes later Bella was still crying, and my motherly radar told me to go check on her. I went into her bedroom, wrapped my arm around her, and felt three elbows on her left arm.

I screamed to Mark, "She's broken her arm! Oh my God!"

I'd put my sweet child to bed with two broken bones because she couldn't tell me she was hurt.

You can have a million dollars in your pocket and still not be certain how to best care for your child with autism. Add to that the definition of a "spectrum disorder" with more flavors than Baskin Robbins, and you learn quickly that autism presents itself differently in each child.

What works for one child might be of little use to the next. I've found this to be true within my own family. Mia responds well to a scientifically proven behavioral therapy used to manage autism called applied behavior analysis, or ABA, as does Bella. Gianna does not. All three girls have food allergies common to people with autism: a strong reaction to gluten, the protein in wheat, oats and rye; and casein, the protein in milk. They also must avoid soy.

If Bella ingests gluten or casein, she doubles over in pain, bites her fingers bloody, and screams endlessly as pain ravages her GI system. Yet Mia and Gianna can have a slice of pizza every so often, although they are gluten- and casein-free 98 percent of the time. *Discover* magazine ran an article in April 2006 about the brain-gut connection in autism, work based on the groundbreaking research of a neurologist in Boston named Dr. Martha Herbert. My children's autism and their food issues are interconnected. Studies prove it. I've been saying so for years solely on the basis of the girls' behavior. I hope more doctors and educators discover that something as basic as food can grossly affect an autistic child's behavior.

Parents and teachers of spectrum kids need a large bag of tricks and a healthy respect for changing course on a dime. If Plan A fails, be ready to move on to Plan B—and don't get discouraged if you find yourself at Plan Q before you get results. I will let you in on a secret: the results are worth the work and the wait. There is nothing more satisfying than watching an ASD child achieve a new success—big, small, and everywhere in between.

The ASD diagnoses have altered our family's course in many ways, but they will not destroy us. I suppose you could say autism has made us three times stronger as a family. It has introduced us to a new family, including other parents of kids on the spectrum, dedicated doctors who risk professional criticism to help their young patients, remarkable therapists, and teachers who work day in and day out to get skills into my girls. These are some of the finest people I have ever met.

There are men and women across the country who are willing to fight for better schools, improved medical care, laws that include our kids, and insurance that covers autism treatment. These folks are trailblazers and iconoclasts, unafraid of stirring up controversy if it means a better life for our kids, for my kids.

I really need to work on my response to the dental receptionist, the dry cleaner, the neighbor who tells me "I'm sorry" when I say my child has autism. There is no need to apologize to me. You didn't do anything wrong. Neither did my girls.

I hope one day we'll have real answers as to why my three girls carry an autism diagnosis. I think their father and I, along with the parents of the one-in-150 kids currently being diagnosed, deserve answers, not apologies however well intended.

4

PATIENCE—THE LEAST IMPORTANT "SUPER POWER"

[BY KRISTIN KAIFAS-TENNYSON]

(A professional educator with more than fifteen years of experience, Kristin Kaifas-Tennyson works with autism spectrum disorder children as an administrator at an alternative school in Cincinnati. —RP)

Whenever people ask what I do for a living and I tell them I work in the special education field, their typical response is something along the lines of, "Wow! You must have a lot of patience."

This reaction used to bug me, probably because part of me wished I had more of it. But beyond that, the "lot of patience" comment raised a number of questions and for me conjured up the image of a dynamic superheroine.

Why do most people assume I have such an abundance of patience? With more, would all the children who cross my professional path make monumental gains? If I channeled this virtue of patience into, say, a Wonder Woman–like golden lasso, twirled it three times, and roped a challenging child during a difficult moment, would both our lives become easier and more fulfilling?

Sadly (or not), working with children in the autism spectrum has very little to do with summoning magical super powers, or even patience. Don't misunderstand: patience is an important characteristic for an educator to possess. But it's simply a very small piece of the ultimate puzzle.

My decade-plus of experience, both in the classroom and from my current administrative vantage point, has shown me that gifted teachers make connections with their students—all of their students. Even those who are nonverbal, avoid eye contact, are physically aggressive or disrespectful—the list goes on and on.

These extraordinary teachers break through all barriers (sometimes in spurts) and form trusting relationships with each and every child. They enable a child to feel confident enough to express himself without fear of rejection. They find ways to help the child explore who he is and who he is capable of becoming within a safe, encouraging atmosphere.

They are able to see each child as a unique individual who deserves the opportunity to convey his true self in a nonjudgmental environment. They allow the child to be their teacher, allowing continuous growth and development.

All of this can be done by simply making a connection with a child. But how does one truly connect with a child? Especially one with an ASD diagnosis?

Rational Detachment

Working with students anywhere along the spectrum can be a joyous and challenging experience. Making it more joyous than challenging is dependent on the strategies you implement as an educator, the choices you make as an individual, and how you allow perceived negativity to affect you.

Unfortunately, patience, good intent, and caring simply are not enough. You can be an incredibly caring individual but not be a gifted teacher. However, all gifted teachers are caring—caring enough to rationally detach, when necessary.

I know it seems a contradiction to offer the word *detachment* when the focus here is on connection. Rational detachment, by definition, means remaining in a state of self-control and being able to distance yourself enough so you can be productive in providing a remedy to the situation.

In other words, don't take things personally. In the midst of a crisis, or at the very least an upsetting circumstance, you need to have the ability to detach yourself from the situation in a rational way. (Notice that I wrote "detach yourself from the situation," not from the child.)

This is necessary if you are to remain in an evaluative, supportive role, and most important maintain your sanity. You must separate the behavior from the child. If you allow yourself to get all worked up, how can you adequately support this child? How can you fully observe the signals and clues she is giving you that may help solve the mystery of her behavior? How can she trust you to figure it out and make everything OK? How can she feel safe if she does not know that she can count on you to remain calm and dependable during crisis? How can she learn and progress in such an environment?

Use of rational detachment has a major impact on our relationships with our students. Without it, we allow our emotions to overtake the situation. When this happens, we become part of the behavior cycle, prolonging and possibly escalating the behavior of the child, while putting ourselves on a constant roller coaster ride.

In the long run, visiting the educational amusement park results in lack of trust, respect, and a haphazard connection with your students—if you call it a connection at all. Where will you find yourself after a few years of riding the unpredictable emotional rails? More than likely burnt out.

Rational detachment, though a simple concept, can actually be quite difficult to accomplish. After all, you are asking yourself to literally turn off your emotions, at least temporarily, so you can rationally, professionally, and respectfully facilitate the situation at hand. Not only does this take practice, it often requires developing specific strategies. Unfortunately, though many of us understand what rational detachment is and its theoretical usefulness, we don't fully understand how it can enable us to connect with a child until we have directly experienced the outcome.

For this reason, I cannot place enough emphasis on the importance of developing a strategy for yourself that allows you to rationally detach, even under the most stressful and possibly disrespectful or delicate occasions. Let me demonstrate what I'm talking about.

One day, I was late to school because one of my dogs fell and hurt himself. Now, my dog, Bocephius—"Bo" for short—was thirteen years old at the time and, though I'm still in denial, geriatric, according to my vet. It had been a rough year for Bo, with surgery, eye problems, and developing arthritis. He was slowing down, and I often worried about how much longer he was going to be around. Every morning I peeked over the edge of my bed, holding my breath and hoping to see that he was still breathing. When I arrived at school, one of my students on the spectrum, James, asked me why I was late. I explained to him what happened and that I was a little worried about Bo because of his age. James seemed satisfied with my response and went about his day as usual, seeming not to care about Bo and instead finding it more interesting that I was late and had therefore changed his routine. A few days later, however, with an aloof look on his face and little tact, James practically shouted from across the room, "Is your dog dead yet, Ms. Kaifas?"

In my opinion, I had two choices.

Choice A was to take it personally, allow my emotional stress over Bo to get to me, and assume that James was being a rude, insensitive child. I could think to myself, "And after I give so much of myself to James! This is how he repays me?" Then I could respond loudly and angrily to ensure that he understood the intent of my message ("James! That is rude and disrespectful! If you don't have anything nice to say, don't say anything at all."). Of course, I'd fail to explain what actions were rude and disrespectful, thus ensuring that James would be completely confused over my outburst.

Choice B was to begin rationally detaching by taking a deep breath, because I know I'm sensitive about Bo right now. I could evaluate the situation and realize that James must be concerned about me and my dog because it was a few days since Bo's accident and James himself thought to bring up the topic. I could notice that it was possible James might even be having a bit of anxiety over the situation with my dog, because his question came out of the blue and with an intense look on his face—the kind I've seen before when he is anxiety-ridden. I could respond by saying, "Do you mean to ask me, 'How's your dog doing, Ms. Kaifas?'" Then, I would give James the answer and explain the benefits of wording his question differently. Finally, I could relish the fact that I made enough of a connection with James for him to be concerned about my feelings and my dog's well-being, something that he did not always have the ability to display.

I'm happy to say I chose choice B on that day, but I am not so righteous as to be unable to admit that in my earlier years I might have gone with choice A. My ability to choose choice B was based on having developed, by this time in my career, preplanned ways to rationally detach.

Most people think they will simply have the ability to detach when necessary. This is often not the case, however, because it is not natural to turn emotions off like the flip of a switch, especially when one's feelings are hurt. Again, this is why it is so important to predetermine ways to rationally detach. Of course, what is useful to one person is not useful to another, so it is important that you find something that works for you. Then make sure to continuously analyze what you're doing to see if it is actually working or whether you need to try something different.

Detachment Strategies

Personally, I've tried many things. Some were useful, some not. Others were so simple that it seemed ridiculous to even bother with, and some required great effort on my part. Here are a few strategies I've tried that you may find useful. Even if none of these ideas speaks to you, the important thing is that you develop a strategy (or two or three) to actually use when the need arises.

- Leave sticky notes that say "rational detachment!" on your desk and in your lesson plan book and teacher's manuals, or anywhere else you'll look. Sometimes a simple, constant reminder throughout the day is all you need.

- Enlist the help of your co-workers. Come up with a cue to use if one person notices that the other could benefit from rational detachment. Make it positive and agreeable to all. Use it in a helpful way, not as a means of criticism.

- Create a list of phrases or questions to use when a student is in crisis. If done ahead of time, the list will be well thought out, so you don't have to rely on yourself to come up with the best way to phrase things at a time when you know you might be upset. Use these lists until the phrases become automatic for you. Some useful phrases: "It looks like you're really upset," or frustrated, sad, and so on. "What could we do to help you feel better?" (Give suggestions if needed). Or "Are you having a tough day? Would it help to go to the OT [occupational therapist's] room to swing for a while?" Or "Would you like some alone time?"

- Learn, live, and breathe by the thoughts of Rudolph Dreikus, an American psychiatrist and educator. Amid crisis, repeat in your head, "Language is behavior. It is my *job* to figure out what this child is trying to tell me." This way, the focus is on your ability to help solve the problem rather than on getting upset over the name you're being called, or other behavior.

- Notice your reaction to a child's behavior. If you start to feel upset, plan to take a deep breath. While doing so, repeat in your head, "I'm frustrated at my inability to help this child find a solution, not at the child." Then revert to "Language is behavior. It is my job to figure out what this child is trying to tell me."

- Take care of yourself during the school day! If you're not in the right zone, you won't be able to give your students 100 percent. As educators and caregivers, we often forget to take care of ourselves because we focus so much on taking care of others. If our needs are not met, we're unable to properly meet the needs of others. So, unselfishly put yourself first in order to better help those around you. During the school day, make sure you eat when you're hungry. Drink plenty of water throughout the day. Allow yourself enough time to properly plan and structure your classes without killing yourself. Develop a list of quick destressors: taking a deep breath, asking someone else to take over for you for five minutes, taking a quick walk around the building, saying an affirmation, spending a moment with your favorite picture of something you love.

- Take care of yourself outside of the school day. Get enough sleep, and eat healthy. Do things that help you destress, whether it be working out or listening to music. Leave your personal problems at the front door of the school so they don't interfere with your ability to connect with your students and do your job properly.

- Most important, enjoy what you do. Notice the positive in every situation, and build on it.

The Three S's

Successful teachers have the ability to make a connection with their students. These teachers understand that they need to go back to the basics for this to happen. No, I'm not referring to the familiar three R's of reading, writing, and arithmetic. I'm referring to what I call the three S's: *safety*, a *sense of belonging*, and *self-esteem*. To learn, to truly learn, we must first feel safe, feel that we belong, and feel esteemed. Then learning really begins, and it will be evident that a connection has been made.

Unless our basic needs have been met, the human brain functions in a manner that prohibits us from learning at the very least, much less the ability to learn to our fullest potential. These most basic needs, of course, fall along the lines of having adequate food and water . . . and the three S's.

To demonstrate the theory behind our basic needs, recall Abraham Maslow's *Hierarchy of Needs*. If you take a moment to visualize a chart, similar to the one of the basic food groups, you will need to divide it into seven levels. Each level represents a type of need, with the most basic ones that every human being requires falling at the bottom. As well, understand that the needs at a lower level must be met for an individual to fully "graduate" to the next level.

Keeping this in mind, fill in the first five levels of the chart. The lowest level, of course, is basic needs: food, water, and rest. The second level is safety needs: to feel safe, secure, and out of danger. The third level is belongingness and love needs: to love and be loved, have relationships, and be accepted. The fourth level is self-esteem needs: to achieve, gain approval, and have recognition from others for our achievements. It is not until the fifth level that cognitive needs come into play: to know, understand, and explore.

Therefore, before we as educators can expect our students to learn, we must ensure that their lower-level needs are met first. Through meeting these needs as each individual child requires them to be met, opportunities arise that automatically facilitate connecting with the child. In other words, you can develop fantastic lesson plans that focus on reading, writing, and math, but if you haven't met your students' needs for safety, belonging, and self-esteem, you'll only get so far.

Think about it. Consider a school with a high rate of violence. If as a student you're worried that someone is going to beat you up between classes, how well can you focus on the teacher? You can't, because your basic need of feeling safe is unmet.

Now consider other types of safety, those going beyond physical safety. In particular, think about safety by stepping into the shoes of a child in the autism spectrum. If your sensory system is hypersensitive and you constantly feel that people are invading your space, do you feel safe, secure, and comfortable? Or do you constantly feel disrespected, as though you're being attacked? If someone's light touch or accidental bump looks and feels like purposeful physical aggression, do you feel safe, secure, and comfortable, or are you constantly afraid of getting hit? If you can't depend on your teachers to understand you when you strive to let them know you need to use the bathroom, do you feel safe, secure, and comfortable, or are you constantly in fear of the embarrassment of losing control of your bladder?

Under such circumstances, have your safety needs (and for that matter, those of belongingness and self-esteem) been met? If not, how can you truly learn? Accordingly, as educators working with children in the spectrum, we need to reconsider how we define safety. When most of us think of arranging a safe classroom, we typically focus on things that could cause physical harm to our students. We make sure there are no sharp edges left uncovered or cords lying carelessly across the floor to trip over. We practice fire drill safety procedures, and naturally, as all good teachers do, we immediately teach our students how to properly hand a friend scissors. (Scissors closed, with the blades in your hands, while you hand the receiver the end that you place your thumb and pointer finger in. Then wait for the receiver to say "thank you" before releasing the scissors.) Sometimes, however, our thoughts do not go beyond this physical type of safety.

Working with children in the spectrum (or with any type of disability, for that matter), we need to pay particular attention to what makes a specific child feel safe, as if she or he belongs and is esteemed. The problem, of course, is that you usually can't just go up to your student and say, "So, Ryan, tell me. What do I need to do to help you feel safe so you can learn to your optimal capacity? How can I assist in making you feel you're part of the group? And your self-esteem . . . let's discuss ways to improve it."

Instead, you must proactively try to experience your classroom and school as your students may be experiencing it. You must do your best to try to see and feel things as your students might. You must take all of the information you've gathered from your students' and parents' files and combine it with your observations to formulate questions, which you have to ask yourself—but answer through your students' eyes:

- Am I providing enough consistency and structure for this child so he is able to predict what I'm going to do next or how I'm going to respond to a situation? To what degree does he need to know what is next—every five minutes, or every hour? Will this decrease some of his fears and anxieties so he can feel safe?

- What is the size of my classroom? Is it possible that it appears to be as big as the Grand Canyon? Do I need to reduce the size of the space we are using for this child to feel safe and comfortable? Is the space too closed in? Does it need to open up more for this child to feel safe and comfortable?

- What are this child's known fears? Is it possible that any of those fears will be generalized to my classroom? If so, what changes can I make to eliminate those fears so this child can feel safe and belonging?

- What sensory needs does this child have? Is she constantly in fight, flight, or fright mode? Is the environment and child's schedule set up to reduce sensory overload, or to aggravate it? What sensory strategies do I need to integrate into this child's day for her body to remain in a comfortable state? How often do I need to implement these strategies so this child can feel safe and as though she belongs?

- Have I put in place the visual supports that this child requires to understand the skills I'm presenting, and to follow a routine? Have I done it to the extent that this child feels esteemed and safe enough to make mistakes in front of others?

- Have I given this child the means to communicate his needs to me so he feels comfortable knowing that I'll be able to understand him when he requires something, or when he's in crisis?

- Are there opportunities available for this child to successfully establish and maintain friendships? Have I established a community that allows all students to feel they belong?

- Have I broken down tasks enough and in such a way that this child will successfully accomplish skills throughout the day? Does this child feel esteemed, as though he is making progress and doing something meaningful?

- Do I challenge this child? Do I offer experiences that allow her to grow? Do I have high expectations and build supports around her, or are my expectations too low? Am I enabling this child, or am I building her self-esteem through enhancing independence?

In my experience, focusing on the three S's is critical to student success. Not only will the three S's have an impact on your students' ability and rate of academic progress but they will help students develop personal connections with others, enhancing their social skills.

As educators, sometimes our focus is so streamlined toward academics that we forget that they can't come about unless the three S's are there. Think in terms of math. Would you attempt to teach a child to do algebra problems before teaching basic facts? Of course not. We clearly understand that these other skills are prerequisites to being able to successfully solve algebra problems.

It is the same way for learning in general. There are prerequisites that must be met for productive and efficient learning to occur: safety, a sense of belonging, and self-esteem. Besides, social skills are a critical area of development for all students, especially those in the spectrum.

I believe developing social skills is equally important as—dare I say, more important than—academic skills. After all, without adequate social skills our children cannot develop functional and satisfying relationships with others. Without social skills, people cannot develop friendships or other personal relationships. They may not be able to function at a job if they can't get along with others and demonstrate appropriate social behaviors. If they don't have friends, intimate relationships, a job, are they going to be happy and able to reach their fullest potential?

Corry is a twelve-year-old student at my school. He is intelligent, energetic, and caring. He also has been diagnosed with Asperger's Syndrome and can be impulsive, obsessive, and unaware at times. He so badly wants friends, and in particular he wants to be the best of friends with another student. He doesn't always feel he belongs, and he often does things that are counterproductive to achieving his goal of developing friends.

One day, one of his teachers brought him down to my office, quite upset because Corry had just called her a name and made fun of her. (If memory serves, it was something to the effect of calling her a "wuss" and telling her she "sucked" at the game they were playing.) As Corry and I discussed what happened, he quite openly told me what he did. With the help of some more reflective questioning, he determined that the reason he said those things wasn't because he meant them but rather because he was trying to make everyone else laugh. He wanted their attention and thought they would think he was cool if he acted that way.

Through even more reflection, we determined that though his goal was to be cool and get friends, he did not achieve it. In fact, he did just the opposite. He realized not only that he was disrespectful but also that the other kids thought he was being rude, not cool. Finally, with desperation in his voice, he blurted out, "Just tell me how to do it! What do I need to do to be cool? I just want the other kids to like me." Then he actually said, "All I want is to belong."

What did this interaction with Corry teach me? Well, for starters, that I needed to make sure I continued to rationally detach, because my heart broke just listening to him. But then what? Belonging—a sense of belonging. Despite all of our previous efforts of scheduling Corry in a social skills class daily, scheduling him in another class that focused around community building, and emphasizing personal social skills goals, we still did not find a way to help him feel as if he belonged.

Implementing Strategies That Lead to Connection

"Great!" you say, "but how do I really do all that? I mean, if I don't have a child's attention, or I can't adequately communicate with him, or if his sensory system is constantly out of whack, how can I even get a child to participate in activities?"

The first step in answering the connection question is simple. Though each child is unique and requires specific interventions to meet his or her own needs, there are a few strategies—two in particular—that should automatically be considered for all children in the spectrum. These strategies are the ones that make or break not just your students' academic success but your ability to connect with each child as an individual, as well as his or her ability to develop other social relationships.

STRATEGY ONE: SATISFY EACH CHILD'S SENSORY NEEDS

Having a child go to occupational therapy once or twice a week is not going to cut it. You are going to need to learn how to follow through with and *integrate* sensory strategies into your classroom all day long. If you don't, your students will be in fight, flight, or fright mode most of the time.

If this is the case, you'll never get to academics, let alone make a connection with the child. Of course, you need to work closely with an occupational therapist but you really need to school yourself in sensory integration, becoming as much of an expert on the subject as possible. This is extremely important; it's highly unlikely that learning about sensory integration was part of your college experience when you were taking classes to help prepare you to teach, yet it's one of the most necessary components to address in a classroom with children in the spectrum. (The book *How Does Your Engine Run? A Leader's*

Guide to the Alert Program for Self-Regulation, by Mary S. Williams, is an excellent resource.)

You may need to—OK you're just going to *have* to—throw many traditional classroom procedural techniques out the window. After all, "criss-cross, applesauce" doesn't get you very far with a child who can't sit still for more than five seconds. You might have to give up on that and allow the child to sit on a therapy ball so she can stay in one place yet bounce and get the movement and input that her body needs. By doing so, you will probably find that her attention increases and some of her behaviors may diminish so she participates more with the group.

Along with your student's OT, develop a sensory diet, or a menu of types of sensory input, scheduled and unscheduled. By doing this, you can have an impact on many areas of development, some of which will greatly improve the child's academic capabilities and some of which will affect social skill capabilities, allowing more connections and relationships to take place.

Some examples of sensory input that are easily used:

- Bounce lightly on a therapy ball

- Bounce on a minitrampoline

- Suck through a straw, particularly thick liquids such as a shake or applesauce

- Suck on tart, bitter, or other flavorful candies that wake up the mouth

- Chew bubble gum (usually, the harder the gum, the better!)

- Crunch on pretzels, animal crackers, chips

- Use cinnamon and mint scents in the classroom to wake up the body

- Use vanilla and lavender scents in the classroom to calm the body down

- Swing

- Roll the child like a sandwich with a therapy ball

- Compress the shoulders with hand pressure

- Do somewhat heavy work, such as carrying a few textbooks

- Do chair or wall pushups

- Use a weighted vest

- Use body socks

- Listen to therapeutic music

- Do rope pulls

- Crash into mats or pillows

The list can go on and on. The important thing to remember is to work with your student's OT to develop ways of helping with sensory regulation that are both effective for that particular child and easily used within the constraints of your classroom and school. Many of my suggestions can be used or implemented while you are teaching, or they can be set up in sensory stations for children to use as needed throughout the day. You may even find that you start planning group and individual sensory breaks into your lesson plans, which definitely enhances everyone's learning.

One year, I had a small, multiage classroom of five students in grades K–2. All were boys, and the children had a variety of diagnoses: Jason had bipolar disorder and attention deficit hyperactivity disorder (ADHD); Aaron had autism; Tommy had a hearing impairment, ADHD, and oppositional defiant disorder (ODD); Stephen had autism, ADHD, and a cognitive disability; and Carl had a learning disability, ADHD, and ODD. All of them had some type of sensory needs.

Every day, after unpacking, we gathered in a circle for about fifteen minutes for morning meeting. During this time, we greeted one another, discussed our schedule for the day, got to know one another better through facilitated social opportunities, and worked on building a community within the classroom.

Now, anyone visiting our morning meeting during the first week of school would have seen, quite frankly, utter chaos. Stephen constantly invading others' space, Stephen and Jason talking out, a general lack of attention, arguing between Carl and Jason or between Tommy and Jason, Aaron engaging in arm-flapping or other self-stimulating behavior, and even fighting seemed to be more a part of morning meeting than any actual structured activity. Not one of my students had the ability to sit in the circle for fifteen minutes, let alone pay attention, participate, or socialize with classmates.

By the end of the first week of school, I didn't know if I would make it through the next month, let alone the whole school year. Talk about needing sensory input! I was on sensory overload from just being in the room, and I was the teacher. All of our problems—well, almost all of them—were fixed by a few therapy balls, deep compressions, "brain food," "chewies," water bottles, therapeutic listening music, and strategically planned movement activities. A carefully planned sensory diet allowed us to function as a cohesive group.

If you had visited our morning meeting toward the end of the first quarter, by contrast, you would have seen Carl sitting on a therapy ball, Jason lying over another therapy ball while using brain food to help him self-regulate, Tommy with headphones using therapeutic listening music, Stephen sitting in a chair with a weighted pillow and a water bottle, and Aaron bouncing on a third therapy ball while using a chewy. You would also have seen children who were able to participate in the circle for the entire fifteen minutes, interactions and exchanges between Carl and Jason, Aaron sharing ideas, and actual friendships being developed. In fact, this became everyone's favorite time of the day. Never underestimate the power of meeting the sensory needs of your students!

STRATEGY TWO: CHANGE YOUR TEACHING STYLE TO THAT OF YOUR STUDENTS' PRIMARY LEARNING STYLE: VISUAL

As a teacher, you probably have a preferred style of teaching with one primary modality. More often than not, this method is auditory. Even when we're not teaching, we typically give most of our directions, encouragement, and discipline verbally. The problem with doing this while working with children in the spectrum is that typically their primary means of learning is visual. As well, many children in the spectrum have some type of language processing need that requires support beyond simply using the auditory.

So when setting up your classroom and developing your lesson plans, procedures, and daily routines, consider which visual elements should accompany them. To begin with, assume a high level of visual support is called for, almost to the extent that you might provide to a nonreading, hearing-impaired child. Indeed, consider visual supports in all of these areas (and others):

- Visual schedules, so children are aware of the daily schedule (organize the written or picture schedule vertically)

- Class schedules that list all of the activities for a specific class

- Visuals to indicate starting and stopping points with activities, because many children in the spectrum have difficulty determining when to start and stop (this is why we often see repetitive behavior, doing a puzzle or reading a story over and over)

- Sign language in "one-word" increments to give simple directions and reminders (good signs to start with are "stop," "wait," "quiet," "sit," "stand," "listen," "come")

- Visual pictures or written words as labels throughout the classroom to help indicate where items belong

- Picture or word choice boards for areas you are working on with a child (if a child is struggling with self-regulation, have a visual choice board of sensory activities he can use; if struggling with managing frustration, have a similar board of activities he can do when frustrated)

- Visual choices for answers to comprehension questions

- Visual choices or choice boards to help promote social activities (instead of giving just free time, have visual choice boards that students can use to help choose what they are going to do and who they are going to play with)

- Visuals to assist with school rules and classroom procedures (you may have a "raise hand" picture on the child's desk or on your chalkboard that you can point to as a reminder; use a "wait" card that flips over to a "my turn" card when a child is learning turn taking)

- Social stories, with or without pictures, to promote social skills

- Social videos that include the student to promote social skills

- A list of conversation starters for use in various situations

- A "Time Timer" (visual timer that shows a red block to indicate time; the red block diminishes as each minute goes by)

- Visual (written or picture) check-off lists to indicate that items are done

- Task analysis to teach a skill while using pictures to accompany each step (Boardmaker computer software by Mayer-Johnson is an excellent tool for making all of your visual picture schedules, charts, cards, and other materials)

This list can be expanded, so whatever you're doing and wherever you are, think about whether or not you have supplied visual supports to your students in the spectrum.

Visual supports can be offered in many ways: written language, picture symbols, drawings, photographs, or videos. You'll be amazed at the results you get. Children who were unable to follow simple directions can do so easily. Children who had a meltdown over work can find success with the amount of work they complete. Children who wandered during free time have direction and purpose.

Byron was a bright, energetic first grader in the autism spectrum at my school. He had the biggest smile in the classroom but the most difficulty staying seated and in his space while the group was working. Consequently, we gave Byron two easy visual supports: a carpet square to sit on, which gave him a visual marker for his personal space; and a four-inch-square laminated card with a picture of a person sitting and the word *sit* underneath it. When Byron would start to get up, we simply signed the word *sit* or pointed to his sit card. Before we knew it, Byron was not just staying in his own space but sitting through the length of activities. At that point, we were able to move to higher-level skills so Byron could participate and socialize with the group.

Though I still keep my magic "patience lasso" handy, I've learned to keep a few other tools around as well: rational detachment, the three S's (again: safety, sense of belonging, and self-esteem), and strategies that incorporate sensory regulation and visual supports at all times.

I know these strategies and tools work. I see it every day, when Erwin initiates saying "hello" to me as we pass in the hallway; when Corry shares his fears; when Cameron is in a meltdown but allows me to help him regroup; when alumni students choose to come back as high schoolers to volunteer in the school; and when Roger, a former student, names his first child after the school.

Is there better proof than that?

5

NORTH OF THE
BORDER

[BY GAY AND DENNIS DEBBAUDT]

(Gay and Dennis Debbaudt are the very proud parents of Brad, in his midtwenties, diagnosed with ASD well before autism became a mainstream topic of discussion. They have handled his diagnosis with diligence, compassion, and humor. —RP)

Pillows, towels, and blankets? Check!

Favorite foods and beverages? Check!

Flashlights, camera, radio, and batteries? Check!

Our predawn packing completed, we were ready to spend a long weekend at our friend's across-the-border cottage on a Georgian Bay Island.

The trip in our very cool van would take about five hours. We were taking the back road route along the eastern shore of Lake Huron to avoid the heavy traffic on Ontario's Highway 401. So we drove north from Detroit to Port Huron, where we would cross into Canada at Sarnia via the Blue Water Bridge.

Welcome to Canada

About fifty minutes into our journey, the brilliant morning sunshine illuminated the beautiful view from the bridge. On our left, Lake Huron's green waters mingled with the clear blue of the Saint Clair River as it flowed under us from the right. Traffic was light on this crisp, clear early summer morning. The Canada Customs and Immigration post came into view as we passed into Canada at the bridge's midspan.

Growing up in border city Detroit, one becomes adept at entering Canada and passing customs. At Detroit-Windsor customs, for example, you wait your turn, pull up to the inspection booth when directed, and answer the standard questions, which are typically directed to the driver's side of your vehicle.

"Citizen of what country?" "Where are you going today?" "Business or pleasure?" "How long will you be in Canada?" "Are you bringing in any weapons?"

We've heard the phrase hundreds of times.

Canadian customs at the Port Huron-Sarnia border was different. You had your choice of pulling up near the booth from either the right or left. There, Canadian customs agents step out of the booth and approach your vehicle, presumably to get a better look.

We pulled the van up to the left and stopped. We were all wide awake and ready for Canadian customs Q and A.

Our van at the time featured two captain's chairs in front and full carpet in the back. The front passenger side was the only appropriate place to plant six-year-old Brad's comfortable child seat. He loved the lofty view.

A pretty, young Canada customs agent popped out, resplendent in her crisp, blue uniform and neat dark blue bowler that featured a gold maple leaf hat badge insignia.

Brad's window was already down for the fresh air when she approached our van at the passenger side window. As she leaned in with a look of confidence about what we expected would be the standard questions, Brad reached out with his right hand and gave her left breast a full and firm grab. Her face showed surprise and embarrassment and was as red as the maple leaf pin on her uniform top.

She lurched back, and quickly waved us through without a question being asked.

Welcome to Canada!

We laughed all the way to our destination.

We'll never know why Brad innocently groped the customs agent. He'd never done anything like that before, and hasn't since. Was it the sudden invasion of his personal space? Was he reaching out to touch her shiny pin lapel?

Of course, the agent couldn't have known Brad was riding shotgun with a diagnosis of autism. It was something we had discovered only three years before.

First Steps

That was spring 1987. After months of testing that included videotaped play, games, examinations, and interactions with the staff, we were given an appointment to come to the office without Brad.

The very nice psychiatrist at Children's Hospital of Michigan in Detroit announced Brad's autism in a friendly, matter-of-fact manner: "Your son has autism. There's no cure. He'll always seem odd or different to others, but with special help he can learn some independence skills and, hopefully, learn to read and write. He'll have difficulty accepting changes in his routine. He has a fascination with letters and numbers and will take great comfort in these things since they will never change. There's no way to determine what life will be like for him as an adult, but you, as parents, can make a big difference in how he learns and accepts his autism."

The doctor suggested we find out all we could about autism and get involved with a support group. He recommended that we take advantage of any special programs the school system offered.

We both grieved and cried during that drive home. It wasn't the first time we had heard the word *autism* associated with Brad. Family and friends familiar with the symptoms of the diagnosis had hinted at it. But you can't really prepare yourself for the day you hear the words spoken with certainty.

Nonetheless, we quickly reached the conclusion that our attitude toward our young son and his condition in life could make a big difference. It was, after all, his life we were talking about, not ours. We vowed in the car that day to do all we could to educate ourselves and our son about autism. We would find a way to give him every opportunity to live a full, independent life. Autism or not, we would show the world to Brad and show Brad to the world.

We told him he had autism as soon as we got home that day. We explained we would help him learn to communicate and help other people understand his autism. As a three-year-old, we couldn't know what he took in from the conversation, but we've spoken openly about autism in front of Brad ever since. We told Brad that it's OK to have autism and OK to tell other children and adults that he has autism. We also let him know that it would always be his choice to tell others.

Reaching Out

We contacted our local chapter of the Autism Society of America and started attending local meetings, especially keen to connect with the parents and families of teens and young adults. We wanted and needed a glimpse into Brad's future. It felt good to be with other families who had been there and hear from the teachers and therapists who worked with them. They kindly shared their experiences and advice. We learned that no two persons who have autism are alike, yet they have many experiences in common, including educational and therapeutic choices.

The Internet wasn't available to us at the time. Autism bookstores back then could feature only enough materials to fill a card table. So, it was learn what you can when and where you can.

We connected through the support group with a savvy Detroit public schools autism consultant. While discussing Brad's future, she offered us some sage advice: "Don't worry about anything he's doing now that won't matter when he's an adult. Worry now about what he's doing that will get him in trouble when he's an adult."

Great advice, we thought. Don't sweat the small stuff.

Of course, we took advantage of all the speech and language, physical, sensory, and occupational therapies offered by school district professionals. We supplemented that with private therapy. We desperately wanted Brad to be able to understand the words and ideas that came from the pages of books and the mouths, facial expressions, and body language of others.

We also invested a lot of patience and time with pediatricians who treated his symptoms of a bad rash, diarrhea, and weight loss without looking for the cause. On a recommendation from a friend, we went to see her holistic doctor, who recognized it as a tough intestinal yeast infection. He told us that *Candida albicans* infections were not uncommon for children with autism. Brad was put on a sugar-free, yeast-free diet; we joined him to make it easer for him. Brad was also put on active cultures, acidophilus, and bifidus. His symptoms improved within days, and to our surprise so did his behavior and learning progress. We all developed an affinity for cashew butter on rice cakes.

We spent money we hadn't earned yet to give him auditory integration therapy.

We subscribed to the belief that if a treatment, therapy, or educational program didn't hurt him—and if we believed it might help—then it was OK to give it a try. It's OK to make a mistake. We also came to understand that it was all right to stop something that wasn't working.

Patience is a concept we've always believed in. We were patient with the therapies and specialized teaching methods, and Brad was patient with his parents' and teachers' skills in making them work for him. Developing patience with and for each other is not only a concept but truly a virtue.

Brad needed an aide during those early years in school, but this was something we could not afford. So Gay set aside her career as a professional seamstress to take a job as a teacher's aide for another classroom to free up an aide for Brad at the Montessori school he attended from kindergarten through sixth grade. This allowed Brad to have an early one-on-one teacher's aide and gave Gay and the teaching staff the opportunity to quickly identify and address learning and social issues before they became too onerous to resolve.

The Learning Curve

Our children may be more resilient than we think. It's not easy to gauge progress when you're involved in a day-to-day learning process, and it doesn't come fast; but it does come. Progress didn't happen overnight. With parents, teaching staff, and especially Brad all working together, we made it work.

He learned to read the books he loved to have read to him as a youngster. With help from school and private specialists, his shaky, left-handed handwriting improved. He slowly learned to take turns on the playground. He excelled in art and music. He was learning how to learn. Of course, we were all thrilled.

Then we remembered what the autism consultant told us just after receiving the diagnosis. Was the academic learning the big stuff, or the small stuff? Were we focusing on the academics too much? Would it matter during his adult life if he added two plus two and came up with five? After all, we hire accountants to prepare our taxes and rely on the talents of many others for the services of a lifetime.

Were we worrying enough about the things he was doing now that would get him into trouble as an adult? Would it be acceptable, for example, for him to grope a customs officer? hug a stranger? cut in front of a husband to talk to the man's wife? How would he react when a police officer suddenly appeared on the scene? Would he understand a sexual come-on? Would he be able to tell the difference between friend or foe?

Perhaps this was the big stuff after all!

To improve his community life skills education, Brad learned how to ride a bike and stay on the sidewalk. We practiced crossing the street, teaching the significance of street signs and traffic lights. We took frequent trips on public transportation: buses, trains, even on a plane. We took trips to see family and friends, to restaurants, to ball games at Tiger Stadium, and to shopping malls.

Two incidents, however, made us reflect again on the big stuff.

One was when Brad disappeared while we were visiting Dennis's brother's house. He was found after a frantic fifteen-minute search, only after my brother's neighbor stepped out of her house and with a grin on her face called out to us, "Is this yours?" as she displayed our young son proudly in her arms.

It turned out that as we were greeting my brother's family on their front porch, our little guy walked through their house and went out the back door and down three yards into the back door of the neighbor's house. The neighbor found a complete young stranger in her family room playing contentedly with her own kids' toys.

Walking the Line

Another important incident happened during one of those shopping trips as we were stopped and quizzed by mall police on suspicion of child abduction. This was what other shoppers had observed and reported to police when they saw Dennis struggling with Brad during a behavioral meltdown inside a toy store.

These incidents rang a bell for us. What would the police have done if they arrived to find Brad as an adult alone, throwing a tantrum in a store? What would happen if, as an adult, he wandered into an unsuspecting neighbor's home? Would the neighbors grin and bear the intrusion from a strange man? Probably not. It would be more likely for police to respond.

What this meant for Dennis was an unexpected career choice: educating law enforcement about autism. Researching, reporting, and producing training videos and tools about the interactions between children and adults who have autism and law enforcement professionals is now a reality for Dennis.

For Brad, these life skills lessons started early. We created simple, printed rules that we signed and posted on the refrigerator:

- You can't push or hit other people.

- You can't destroy your property or the property of others.

- You can't say you are going to hit or destroy property.

Brad asked what would happen if he did. We could have said, "Oh, you won't be able to play with your favorite toys or watch your favorite video." Instead we remembered the big-stuff advice (what if he did this as an adult?).

Our answer reflected the adult reality of such behavior: "You'll go to jail," we replied.

An eight-year-old, Brad asked questions about jail. We told him in plain terms that jail is a place where you have no choices about what you do, what you eat, where you can go. We offered to take him on a tour of a jail. We even drove by a correctional facility. He saw the concertina-wire-topped fences and decided that he didn't need a tour.

Of course, we didn't hound him or pound this into him. We didn't remind about the rules when he got into a little trouble. We talked about the rules occasionally, never in the heat of the moment, and included ourselves as people who needed to follow them. He got it, and he follows them religiously to this day.

Developing Empathy

We were married at downtown Detroit's historic Saint Bonaventure Chapel, a nineteenth-century building located little more than a stone's throw from the Detroit River. This was also where Brad was baptized. The remains of Father Solanus Casey, Detroit's healing priest from the 1930s through the 1950s, are interred in the chapel. The Roman Catholic Church is considering Father Solanus for sainthood.

When we told Brad about the chapel's midweek, early-afternoon healing service, he wanted to go. We attended the healing services for about a year. After a short prayer, the informal service offered the opportunity for those in attendance to raise their hands and talk about spouses, sons, daughters, relatives, and friends in need and ask for the group to pray for them. Brad preferred to sit away from us during these services. He wanted to meet new people; he did, and he was very popular.

Sometimes Brad would bravely raise his hand to ask for a prayer for a new friend he was sitting next to. As the priest came around to pray for each parishioner, Brad would touch the priest and the person's shoulder next to him. This would create a special, physical web of people praying for one another. We could actually see the web from where we were sitting, oftentimes teary-eyed. Brad is very spiritual. Just short of a miracle, the whole experience helped improve his communication and social skills. There is nothing like the power of prayer.

Academic Life

We learned the value of developing good relationships with educators early on. Brad wanted to do well in school, but challenges—ranging from being left-handed to discovering the hidden meaning of stories in his "Great Books" class—were very difficult for him. Classes that required memory skills such as Spanish, Chinese, and music came easier.

It was also very helpful for us to learn the rules of the Individuals with Disabilities Education Act (IDEA) and the in and outs of working with educators to develop Brad's annual individual education plan (IEP).

While Gay was occupied with Brad's everyday care and the nightly rituals of homework, Dennis went to IDEA and IEP parent education classes. As a result, we gained a better understanding of the rules and realized that parents and educators truly have the same goals in mind: the best interests of students with disabilities.

Sure, there were contentious meetings over the years. But the training and positive partnerships that developed gave both sides to the ability to dismantle or work around any roadblocks. We learned that what's reasonable and fair for everybody in a meeting room is often what's workable and doable in the classroom.

When it was time to move on from Montessori, we wanted and needed Brad's input about where to attend high school. Brad chose a public school for students with autism. He was intrigued with the idea of attending a school where no one would tease him for being different, a school where, as he put it, "They know about autism." Brad had never attended a center-based school, but the reasons for his choice were sound. He would go to a school where they got autism.

During a visit to the school while class was in session, Brad asked Gay to come meet a new friend. Brad's friend was sitting on a bench in the hallway as school was letting out. As Brad and Gay approached him, he looked away from us and rocked back and forth. Brad said, "I would like you to meet my mom, Gay."

While still looking away and rocking, to Gay's surprise this young man extended his hand to shake hers. Brad later told us his friend didn't speak at all, but he understood everything. The teachers knew this all too well. They taught all subjects and social skills in the belief that their students would eventually get it—and they did.

Brad learned the value of patience, empathy, and sympathy. He was neither the first nor, more importantly, the last person to get it socially or emotionally. By making friends with other students with autism, his personal understanding of the condition quickly expanded. He learned the lessons of patience, empathy, sympathy; he learned to advocate for himself.

In addition to academics, the school also offered life skills and vocational opportunities. Brad worked at a nursery and a hospital. He tried things he had resisted in the past, such as field trips to Toronto, museums, and the state Capitol. He found out he could have fun with people who knew about and accepted his autism. Brad's three-year experience at this school broadened his vocational, social, and academic horizons beyond anything we could have imagined.

Sharing the Wealth

Brad's last two years of high school were in an inclusive environment in Florida. Although the new kid, he was one of only a few students with autism who had ever attended that school.

We had moved to a fast-growing region of the state and into a school district where autism was still something they were learning about. Since Brad was in an inclusive setting, we and district administrators—of course, with Brad's approval—agreed that students and staff would benefit from an autism awareness inservice session. We feel strongly that informed students are more likely to accept a peer who has autism.

We offered to talk with Brad's classmates about autism and the fact that Brad had it. Our offer was accepted.

We were given about fifteen minutes to explain autism and tell a little something about Brad to the other students. We knew from experience that to get accommodation for something people have to know that they need to accommodate. We knew that Brad required some extra eyes and ears to keep him safe on the campus. We also knew that isolation due to disability is a reality families live with every day.

So, to create some accommodations and hopefully a friend or two for Brad, we made isolation owing to autism a part of our talk.

To explain isolation, the class was asked how times over the last month a friend had dropped in on them or given them a call at home, or how many times they saw a friend in the community and hung out for a while.

One of the girls who raised their hand responded by saying, "Oh, maybe, like . . . a hundred." Many others nodded in agreement. The male response was summed up by one fellow who said, "I dunno, maybe ten or fifteen."

The class was told that Brad had had about ten or fifteen contacts like that *in his lifetime*. Social isolation is a reality for many young people with autism. Social contacts that aren't a result of an IEP meeting or plan developed to get peers to interact with them, that is, naturally occurring social contacts, are hard to come by.

The talk did the trick. His classmates learned something about autism about someone in their midst who had it. With disclosure, Brad's social contacts increased.

A gang-color-wearing classmate took an interest in Brad. When Dennis learned of this, he approached the young man at a school basketball game. The fellow told Dennis that Brad was an interesting guy. Dennis asked the young fellow to keep an eye on Brad at school, so that other students who didn't know him might not take his autistic mannerisms (standing too close, talking too loud, or not getting what was said to him) as an act of defiance or sign of vulnerability.

He replied, "Don't worry, Mr. D. Nobody's gonna bother Brad." Amazingly, no one did.

Brad took drama class and produced an acclaimed music video seen by many at the school. This got him instant recognition as a cool peer. He became a semicelebrity for that short video. He heard his self-proclaimed nickname, "Fumbles," in the hallway from people he did not know. Student athletes, girls, and others became school friends.

Into the Future

Brad's credits from up north were approved at his new school, and he took night classes and worked with tutors to be able to pass the requirements necessary to earn his high school diploma. Though never easy, and always exhausting for him, all those years of hard work finally paid off.

In front of thousands at the graduation ceremony, Brad took the walk in his cap and gown for his handshake and diploma, accompanied by applause and cheering from the crowd and the low rumble of "Fumbles!" emanating from his classmates. A proud moment, indeed.

Brad is twenty-four now. He graduated from high school with a 3.2 grade average and recently received his Class B commercial drivers license. He loves listening to and playing on his guitar his beloved jazz and rhythm and blues. One of his goals is to hold the world's record for giving blood. He's been donating every fifty-six days since he turned eighteen.

We are proud of him and all the other resilient autism spectrum children and adults who are giving their best shot at making the most out of everyday life.

We know he couldn't have achieved these goals without the help our family has received from good and caring professional educators that we've had the privilege to form partnerships with over the years.

For all of you, we are extremely grateful.

6

GETTING TO KNOW YOU

Success in ASD Communication and Social Interaction

[BY STEPHEN SHORE]

(In his midforties, Stephen Shore proudly resides in the autism spectrum. He authored three books, is president emeritus of the Asperger's Association of New England, and serves on the board of directors of the Autism Society of America and Unlocking Autism. He has completed his doctoral degree in special education at Boston University and presents his perspective about ASD at conferences all over the world. —RP)

It's always fun and interesting to share what I've learned from my personal experiences with ASD. And personal they are! I love my "job" in life: helping children, teenagers, and adults diagnosed with ASD develop communication skills that make social interactions possible and enjoyable.

I especially enjoy speaking and writing to teachers and parents, sharing my own unique perspective.

My story begins, of course, at the beginning.

After being told that their child had become nonverbal, was considered "too sick" for treatment, and was recommended for institutionalization by diagnosing professionals at a center for children with special needs, my parents took the proverbial bull by the horns and just said "no."

As my mother and father advocated for my placement in the school for the following year, it was up to them to provide what we would today refer to as a "home-based early-intervention program," emphasizing movement, sensory integration, narration, music, and imitation. This was at a time when the concept of early intervention did not exist. Their approach was a hybrid, mostly driven by their own intuition and instincts.

Making the Initial Connection

At first, my mother's attempts to get me to imitate her were met with failure. She then switched tactics and started imitating me. Once she did that, I became aware of her presence in my environment, and my mother was able to begin pulling me along toward greater success in interacting with others. The concept here is that before any successful interaction, instruction, or relationship is going to occur, a connection has to be made with the learner. This goes for all learners, whether nonverbal and firmly planted in the lower end of the spectrum or all the way to a postdoctoral student.

Several years ago, I worked with a child who was particularly challenging to reach and considered difficult to teach. Like many children with autism, he would often reverse pronouns (juxtaposing "me" for "you" is the most common reversal), exhibited a lot of frustration, and had a number of complex self-stimulatory behaviors. One of these behaviors involved flicking his fingers near his eyes while making a clicking noise with his tongue.

During one of those frustrating times, I got really close and imitated this behavior right back at him. Suddenly, he gave me a clear-eyed look and smiled. For the rest of that day we did a lot of good work together (and he didn't reverse his pronouns, at least for a while).

Imitating a child's self-stimulatory and other behaviors can be useful in gaining his attention. Sometimes the child will look at you as if to say "And what do you think you are doing?" Some children may flap with glee, whereas others will seem to get annoyed and try to get you to stop. In all of these cases, a connection has been made. It can be a launching pad to deeper communication, education, and relationships.

Making Deposits into a Child's "Word Bank"

Although I lost my speech at eighteen months, my mother's work on building connections and narrating my activities played a key role in having my speech begin to return at age four. Play-by-play narration, brought to the forefront in "official" ASD intervention strategies by Arnold Miller (Chapter Two), involves maintaining a running commentary—much like an excited sportscaster—of what the child is doing. It is a great alternative to the often ubiquitous "good job!" so often heard when a child completes a task.

The technique of narration works much better for two reasons. First, it is concrete. "Good job" likely means nothing to many children in the spectrum who live in the here-and-now, and it may be too abstract a concept. Second, for nonverbal children and those with limited verbal skills, verbalizing their actions serves to place these words into a "word bank," with the hopes of the child "withdrawing" the words at a later time to attach to activities on his own.

Having a child "self-talk" through an activity using meaningful words is much more useful to the individual than repeating "good job" during and after the completion of activities.

You Say "TomAto," I Say "TomAHto"

Let's look at the "restricted interests" criteria mentioned in the *Diagnostic and Statistical Manual of Mental Disorders IV* (DSM IV-TR). Referring to a salient characteristic of people with autism as "restricted" puts a negative tone on what does not have to be a deficit.

In fact, reframing this characteristic as a "special interest," a phrase coined by ASD expert Tony Attwood, or a "passion" and communicating the positive aspects of this restriction to the person in the spectrum may be just the lead needed for a productive and successful life.

When my speech started to return at age four, the center that had initially rejected me reevaluated. Instead of being considered "psychotic and autistic," I was upgraded to "neurotic." Things were looking up in the world.

At this same time, I started taking apart watches with a sharp kitchen knife. After playing with the faceplate, gears, and hands, I would put the timepiece back together, with no pieces left over and the device still working.

Instead of looking at this as a strange or restricted interest, my parents communicated to me that this was a good and useful passion. In addition to verbalizing that I had this potentially useful mechanical skill, they made additional watches, radios, appliances, bicycles, and other objects available for my disassembly and reassembly.

By age five, most of my verbal communication skills were pretty much normal. However, my entrance to public school kindergarten at age six was a social and academic disaster. There was much teasing and bullying from my classmates. I did not know how to communicate and interact with them socially in a way they expected. By second grade, I was spending hours alone at my desk in school reading my favorite books on astronomy and other topics that piqued my interest.

One day, while reading a stack of astronomy books that were on my desk, a teacher told me that I would never learn how to do math. As a result, I did poorly in this subject and avoided it as long as possible in college. Yet somehow, I was able to learn just enough mathematics, and no more, to teach statistics at the college level in Boston. Had teachers known then what is known today, my special interest in astronomy might have been considered a passion and used to teach me the lower-elementary math skills that I needed at the time.

You say "restricted interest." I say "special interest" or "passion."

I feel compelled to point out here that even if it appears the ASD child or adult in your life does not have a clue about what you are saying, he or she does. Negative comments about learning capabilities are bound to sink in at some level, and this may significantly affect the desire to learn something new.

Special Interests and Passions for a Successful and Productive Life

Making sure a child is aware of strengths (and challenges as well) is important. Doing so plants the seeds of self-determination, or at least gives the child enough self-knowledge to make meaningful decisions about himself or herself in the community. In other words, knowing what you want is the first step in successfully communicating your desires to other people in a way they can understand.

Let's take a look at an example of using a special interest or passion for employment opportunities. In Japan, a parent asked me how her nine-year-old child's special interest in water could be used for work as he transitioned into adulthood. Specifically, this child, who might be considered as being moderately affected with autism, liked to press his finger into a running faucet and spray the water.

Usually, he was very skillful at aiming the stream of water so that it remained in the sink rather than getting all over the floor. But sometimes his water-based activities resulted in minifloods around their house. One aspect that may have driven his interest in spraying water was that he received needed proprioceptive and tactile input from the activity.

Through a translator, I suggested to the mother some opportunities that might fit the boy's interest in focusing water into a high-pressure stream:

- Washing cars

- Washing buildings or sidewalks with a high-pressure hose

- Assisting with water deliveries from a truck and making sure that each customer on the route gets their water when it is due (this child also loved schedules and being on time)

Music for Children with Autism

Teaching children with autism how to play a musical instrument can be a very rewarding way of interacting. Children who are severely affected and nonverbal may discover music as a means of communication. Others may find that music tends to organize their communication. Whatever it is that seems to scramble the speech centers of the brain tends to leave the music areas intact.

In addition to the therapeutic benefits of engaging with music that music therapists strive so hard to achieve, teaching a musical instrument gives the person with autism a real-life skill to interact with others, make friends, and get involved in the community, perhaps by joining a musical ensemble.

Children at all levels of the autism spectrum can learn a musical instrument. Like everyone else, children with autism vary in music ability ranging from having to struggle to play an instrument to becoming professional musicians should they choose to do so.

Finally, music is just plain old fun.

Structuring the Stage for Successful Communication

One does not need to be in the autism spectrum to find the middle and high school experience challenging. With transitioning between classrooms, the advent of homework, changing expectations in the social arena, and adolescence, life becomes much more complex. Additionally, the developmental gap between children with autism and developmental peers continues to increase, creating an even greater sense of difference between the person with autism and peers. However, an often-ignored part of middle and high school that can be of great benefit to those in the autism spectrum, and one that plays right into their special interests, is activities and clubs based on special interests.

In middle school, one of my special interests was music. On noticing my interest, a teacher not only encouraged me but also had me transferred into band. Band was great. The lights reflecting from the instruments in the auditorium were very "stimmy" (my word for "visually stimulating"). At last, I had a structured activity that I could now use to mediate my interaction with other students. In other words, I could talk about the band director or the music to other students, and the routine of the band rehearsals was very predictable. For the first time, I began to form true friendships.

For people with autism to have success in communication and social interaction, gatherings need to be activity-based rather than socially based. For example, although band may work for some students, a computer or chess club can benefit others. Less-structured social activities that typically are more difficult (and not just for those with autism) include holiday dinners with family or friends, school dances, and going to a bar after work for drinks.

At this time, bicycles were also a special interest of mine, leading me to form a bicycle club with an empathic teacher. I was also interested in rock climbing, and I found a teacher who started a rock-climbing club.

A form of paradise for people with autism would be to have all gatherings be activity-based on a special interest and be predictable, resulting in easy communication and interaction. Unfortunately, the world is not always an activity-oriented gathering, so it is important to plan ahead for when more structure and predictability need to be inserted into an event.

For example, a child in the autism spectrum could help set the table, organize a music collection, or assist in some other sort of familiar activity. If you have ever nominated yourself as the dishwasher, you may have given yourself an activity to add structure to a situation.

The ideal goal is to teach persons with autism to insert their own structure into a difficult-to-process social gathering. For example, when at a party I often try to find a piano to play. This way I can structure my interactions with others around making music.

Sometimes there is no piano. For instance, recently my wife and I went to a barbecue dinner party hosted by a friend of hers. My wife, being from China, has many Chinese friends, with whom she converses in Mandarin. When we go to their homes as a couple, if they speak in Chinese it is expected that I will not be able to interact with them as much because my native tongue is not Chinese. As a result, it is perfectly fine for me to leave the conversation after exchanging a few pleasantries in Mandarin to play with their cat, hang out with their children, work on my laptop, or even go home and pick up my wife later on that evening.

This time, however, I had to remain at the party, with no one to talk with and no piano to play. Soon it became clear that even though this was a barbecue, no one knew how to operate the gas grill. I didn't know either but made sure I learned in a hurry. Cooking the food gave me the needed focus and structure to interact with others about cooking.

I then recalled reading in a book on nonverbal communication (another special interest or passion of mine) that punching a guy lightly on the shoulder was a common male bonding activity. The next fellow who approached me that night got a light punch, and soon we were talking. The party was a success.

Self-Advocacy and Disclosure as a Means to Better Communication and Success

A significant challenge in helping a person with autism gain skills in modifying the environment for greater success is helping develop the necessary self-awareness. Educating people with autism in greater self-awareness means helping them understand the characteristics they have that come with being in the autism spectrum. Call it self-disclosure.

At some point, everyone needs to request a change or modification in his or her environment or situation and follow up with explanation or disclosure of why. For example, thanks to visual sensitivities, some people with autism perceive fluorescent lights as many others would a strobe light. If asked to work in a place with this type of illumination, a person having this challenge will have to find a way to request that the supervisor either change the lighting or allow a move to a new location or other accommodation. This is advocacy.

With the advocacy effort comes the need to explain why this change is requested. That's disclosure. Self-advocacy and disclosure are something most people take for granted that they know how to do. People with autism usually need direct instruction both in being aware of their needs and in how to successfully communicate those needs to other people. The prerequisite for self-advocacy is awareness of one's strengths and challenges as a person in the autism spectrum.

TELLING PEOPLE THEY HAVE AN ASD DIAGNOSIS

Sharing knowledge with a person with ASD about his or her "condition" is the first step in being able to self-advocate and disclose.

Ideally there should be no big sit-down talk, telling a person he or she has an autism diagnosis and what it means. Rather, it should be a point of discussion, just as one would talk about having blue eyes or brown hair.

I was lucky in this regard. As early as I can remember, my parents talked about my having autism just as one might discuss how tall I was.

We didn't know much about autism, but it certainly explained a lot of differences I had in school and with making friends. However, most of the time people have to be told they are in the spectrum and what the implications are.

To address this challenge, I have developed a four-step method for letting a person know he's in the autism spectrum. It has proved very useful. Let's take an example of a child with Asperger's Syndrome that I have taught music to over the past eight or nine years, beginning at age five and a half. His parents refused to use the word *autism* in the house because they just knew that with enough intensive activity we could "early interventionize" the Asperger's Syndrome right out of him. By his early teens, his parents realized that the Asperger's was here to stay for a lifetime. I was given the honor of making the disclosure.

STEPS TO DISCLOSURE

What follows are the four steps to disclosing to a person with autism as adapted from my article in the Autism Society of America *Advocate* (2006). With some modification for each individual, these steps can be used to tell someone he or she is in the autism spectrum.

Identify Characteristics Discuss with the person his or her strengths and challenges. I prefer to use the word *challenge* rather than *weakness* because the latter is a static word, whereas the former is active and has the sense that the challenge can be worked through and met.

The discussion with my student began by noting the child's strengths in music, graphic design, and mathematics, followed by an examination of his challenges in the areas of making friends at school, penmanship, and physical education.

Rack Up the Characteristics Work with the person to start delineating the strengths and challenges. Ideally, you will help him realize that his strengths can be used to help accommodate his difficulties.

After sorting out these characteristics, the student and I talked about how he can use his computer-related abilities to help overcome the frustration experienced from the physical act of writing papers and other assignments by hand. He can type them much faster and more neatly than writing them by hand.

Make Nonjudgmental Comparisons Compare the characteristics with those of others to demonstrate that different people have their own strengths and challenges. Examining a potential successful role model, such as those featured in *Asperger's Syndrome and Self-Esteem* (Ledgin, 2004) and *Genius Genes* (Fitzgerald and O'Brien, 2007), with a similar set of characteristics can be helpful.

We examined my student's younger sister for overlapping and differing characteristics. Unlike him, she has great penmanship and makes friends easily. However, they both share an affinity and talent for music. In fact, this child is now teaching his sister to play the piano.

Present the Label Preface discussion of the autism label by noting that there are scientists, teachers, doctors, and others who study the diverse characteristics found in people. You could say, "It just so happens that your characteristics line up with those of people with autism."

After the preface, I told my student that his characteristics line up with what is known as Asperger's Syndrome, followed by a disclosure that I also have Asperger's Syndrome, and perhaps that is why we have gotten along so well over the past eight years. His next statement was, "Can we get to the lesson?" My student had heard enough.

All told, this process took about fifteen minutes. In fact, I told him nothing he didn't know before, save for the label. People with autism, even young children, intuitively know that they have a difference. My student knew he had the strengths and challenges we discussed, but he also realized that accommodations were being made for him as needed.

Revealing the label allowed him to make a cohesive whole out of a sea of characteristics and accommodations. He now also knows that his differences are not because he is stupid or somehow lacking but rather are a function of a neurological difference.

Three weeks later, I met the child's father at work and asked him how his son took the disclosure. His dad beamed, saying, "My son loves having Asperger's Syndrome. He's on the computer learning that he is not alone, how to accommodate for his challenges and to celebrate his strengths."

Armed with sufficient self-understanding, this student is now ready to successfully communicate an advocacy effort for his needs such that others can understand and assist with his requests.

Self-advocacy involves knowing when and how to approach others to negotiate desired goals, and to build better mutual understanding and trust, fulfillment, and productivity. For example, my student now realizes that he can write much better using a computer than by hand. It will be up to him to determine if his challenges of writing by hand significantly affect a situation, and if there is a need for better mutual understanding. In this example, he will need to find a way to communicate his needs to the other person (perhaps a teacher) in a way that can be understood.

The second part of advocacy is to state the reason. My student will now have to offer, as an explanation, information about himself that can be risky to his reputation with the other person. He will have to disclose. However, he can make the choice of partial disclosure, perhaps by just mentioning that he can type much faster and neater than writing by hand and leaving it at that. In this case, there is probably no need for him to disclose that he is in the autism spectrum.

His greater self-awareness constitutes an inner compass to navigate through the tumultuous landscape of his strengths and challenges in order to better communicate with others as part of leading a fulfilling and productive life.

Growing Up

The ability to communicate clearly, and in ways other people can understand, is vital to leading a fulfilling and productive life. For people in the autism spectrum, communication can be especially difficult; direct instruction may be required in areas where most people learn by observation and take for granted.

Good communication can help a teacher, parent, or helper create an initial bond with a person in the autism spectrum. Later on, this bond can be used to teach such persons successful ways to better understand themselves and communicate with others.

The greater self-awareness these people gain can greatly assist in advocating for themselves and in disclosing their autism if there's a need for better mutual understanding and trust.

Targeted interventions, education, support, and friendship directed toward successful communication and connection can enable people with autism to live to their greatest potential.

For me, my diagnosis, special interests, and passion for educating people touched by autism made taking up the challenge to be helpful and empathic an easy decision.

It's my hope you'll be right there with me.

7

LIFE WITH SHAWN

[BY JEANNE LYONS]

(A former elementary school teacher, Jeanne Lyons has devoted most of her adult life to creating opportunities for her son, Shawn, who has a diagnosis of Asperger's Syndrome. She is an accomplished mom, writer, speaker at autism conferences, and musician. We connected not long after I saw her family featured on the television program Dateline NBC. —RP)

In the midst of Advent, a season of great anticipation, our parish at Transfiguration Church hosted a wonderful, professional production of the play *The Littlest Angel*. The large platform on which the altar usually rested became the "stage." The church was swarming with young families. I was full of anticipation, but not the good kind.

Why, oh why, did I have this silly need to do normal, young family things such as take my children to a play? Maybe our five-year-old, Shawn, would urge us to take a specific church pew so he could sit next to the family of a little friend. Maybe he and his little brother, Riley, would be mesmerized by the costumes and actors pretending to be characters in a wonderful story. Maybe they would reenact the story at home for weeks afterward. Maybe as the play started I would relax, breathe a satisfied smile, and just bask in the glow of knowing I was a pretty darn good parent, giving my children a life-enriching, cultural experience.

Oops, wrong family! How could I pretend that we hadn't brought Shawn's Asperger's Syndrome with us, let alone three-year-old Riley's severe regulatory disorder and sensory integration dysfunction?

Of course, we should sit in a spot where we'd be less likely to bother other families. Maybe if my husband, Rory, and I each kept an arm on Shawn, and if Riley fell asleep early in the production, we might not have to leave too long before intermission.

Prior to the first scene, the angel Gabriel had to go and take me out at the knees. Or, I should say the actor playing the angel Gabriel (who obviously didn't have any children of his own) came out and invited all the children to come sit on the floor up close to the stage.

I panicked as Shawn, the human greased watermelon, slipped through our fingers and ended up on the platform steps, front and center, surrounded by a sea of children. There was absolutely no way to get to him without stepping on a multitude of little fingers, and I could feel my blood running cold as I looked up to see that the play had started. My inner voice began to silently scream that this was clearly 100 percent Rory's fault, that I should just pretend everything was OK, smile extra serenely, and sit my helpless self down.

Perhaps Shawn's fidgetiness would eventually propel him like a body surfer floating across the enormous junior mosh pit writhing before me, and he'd miraculously end up back in my anxious arms. "Yeah, right," said my inner voice.

Active, But Odd

"Yeah, right!" I remembered hearing those exact words the week before, at the gymnastics birthday party of the little boy who lived next door. The gymnastics party lady had the kids lined up to climb on one piece of equipment so they could slide across another piece of equipment so they could dangle from a third piece of equipment, while she carefully assisted them one by one, making sure they wouldn't fall. When it was Shawn's turn, he proudly announced that he would instead climb up higher than the other children, execute a diving triple flip onto the trampoline, and then catapult himself up so high that he would dangle from a beam in the ceiling.

The slightly frazzled gymnastics party lady couldn't suppress the sarcastic "Yeah, right!" that slipped past her lips. Of course, Shawn's Asperger's Syndrome kept him from detecting and interpreting the sarcasm in her tone of voice. We had been practicing together, but he had not yet mastered the skill of understanding sarcasm. He took the words "Yeah, right" literally, so with what he thought was her approval he began to do exactly what he had announced he would do. She quickly grabbed him and took him off the equipment. I gently pulled him aside and asked him if he had noticed anything special about the way she had said the words, "Yeah right."

"Oops," he said. "Was she being sarcastic?"

"Yes, she was!" I excitedly answered. "Her tone of voice was sarcastic, so she meant the opposite of what she said."

The poor gymnastics party lady was turning many shades of mortified pink. I was going to ask her to repeat the whole scenario with Shawn, using the same sarcastic tone, to reinforce what Shawn had just learned and give him another chance to respond appropriately. But no, she didn't look anywhere near up to the effort. She did, however, give Shawn a chance later on to do the climbing and dangling thing the other kids had done.

Yes, Asperger's Syndrome has given my son a propensity to think literally. He has had to work hard at remembering to notice, and then being able to recognize, figurative language, and the body language and tones of voice that can give literal words entirely different meanings from those listed in the dictionary.

Meanwhile, back at *The Littlest Angel,* I was grateful that God had sent an angel to help Shawn, who was sprawled out front and center in the mosh pit, trying to self-medicate his sensory challenges by sucking his thumb into oblivion. No one else would have called the little boy next to Shawn an angel. He was even more hyperactive than Shawn. This angel in disguise was helping by making Shawn look good, bless his hyper little heart.

Little Mr. Hoochie Koochie's gyrations were even giving Shawn extra visual stimulation during the dreaded moments of calm on stage.

"Thank you, Lord!" my inner voice whispered. "Now, Lord, would you please just keep Shawn from twirling the hair of the girl on the other side of him?" He loved the feeling of long hair, and many girls at preschool had screamed and cried when he twirled their hair to the point of pulling it hard.

"And Jesus, would you please keep him from kicking anyone?" Because of his "toe walking," Shawn wore braces on his ankles to help keep his Achilles' tendons from tightening to the point of requiring surgery. Shawn didn't have normal awareness of where his body was in space. His arms and legs would often flail about until kicking someone with his extra-heavy, brace-enhanced shoes gave him the proprioceptive input he required to better realize where his arms and legs had wandered.

Of course, other people never appreciated the opportunity to be the ones supplying the proprioceptive input, by being the recipient of a swift kick from Shawn.

"And one more thing, God. During this play, would you please silence any urge Shawn might have to jump up onto the stage and use his booming voice to try to engage any of the actors in a conversation about his favorite interest: carnivorous plants?"

In autism terminology, Shawn was always on the lookout for an adult who might indulge his need to "perseverate" on topics involving his current fixation. Shawn didn't have a shy bone in his body. Tony Attwood, a psychologist from Australia who specializes in the autism spectrum, says folks within the spectrum are not always aloof. Shawn fits beautifully into Attwood's other category, "active, but odd."

The play was very well done, with lots of action to hold the attention of little ones. Although seconds crawled by more slowly than during a ten-hour road trip with the kids, somehow we arrived at the end of the production without any children near Shawn having been accidentally injured or upset. I felt kind of stupid. Why was I unable to recognize that the hours and hours of occupational therapy, physical therapy, and speech therapy with an emphasis on pragmatics, and the efforts of Shawn's one-on-one social-skills coach at school (and most of all, Shawn's valiant efforts) had resulted in some substantial improvements? Needlessly, I hadn't really allowed myself to enjoy the pleasant evening and the rare thrill of successfully doing what "typical" families do.

Just as I was internally beating myself up, I realized that the angel Gabriel was once again speaking to the audience, as the curtain call applause was beginning to wane.

"And now, would you please join us in singing 'Hark the Herald Angels Sing'?" he announced.

"Sure," answered a familiar voice from the front, center section of the junior mosh pit.

I felt every muscle, tendon, ligament, and bone in my body immediately snap back into my usual hypervigilant mode. Shawn sprang onto the stage area and was eagerly reaching for Gabriel's hand. Gabriel had said "Join us" and Shawn was taking him up on it in the literal sense. Shawn was physically joining him on the stage.

"God, it's me again, and this time I'm calling on the red prayer line, the one for emergencies. Please let the lead guy in the angel costume have had semester after semester of training in improvisational theater. Please don't let him try anything really stupid like asking Shawn to go back to his seat. Please let him be playful, kind, and understanding."

Suddenly I noticed that the entire pit was pouring like a flock of lemmings onto the stage area. All the children were holding hands with the cast members and with one another, beaming like spotlights accidentally shining from stage to audience instead of the standard set up of shining onto the stage from the back of the theater. All of these beaming children were belting out a wonderful rendition of "Hark the Herald Angels Sing," with the little ones making up the words and melody as they went along. I suddenly realized that my son Shawn had been the catalyst for this incredibly beautiful moment.

Tears were streaming down the face of every parent in the church. Flashbulbs were snapping and the actors looked indescribably touched. No one in the church would forget the gift of this unexpected tableau of innocence and joy as our children sang with angels, holding their warm hands and admiring their big feathery wings and shimmering white robes.

I gasped at the wonder of it all. Most likely, Rory and I were the only ones who realized that an autism spectrum "difference" had suddenly ceased to be awkward or annoying and was shining like a brief glimpse of the Star of Bethlehem. For a few seconds the world turned, and I witnessed it. I suspected there might be more moments of transfiguration waiting for me in my family's future. I was determined to recognize these fleeting glimpses and cherish each and every one of them.

Fixations

Fixations, perseverations, extremely intense interests—whatever one might call this particular aspect of Asperger's Syndrome, Shawn has had many of them. Some lasted longer than others, but each took up residence in our household like a visiting, long-lost relative.

Every year, our Christmas tree is part holiday decoration and part monument to fixations. Many of the ornaments testify to the fixations of past and present, memorializing those long-lost relatives. One of Shawn's earliest special interests was the study of elephants. This was brought on by the gift of a plush Dumbo that went everywhere with us, lovingly tucked under Shawn's arm, all so cute and typical of any three-year-old.

But our three-year-old not only wanted to collect all sorts of elephants; he also wanted to collect any facts he could possibly learn about them. The teacher in me couldn't help but read lots of elephant books to Shawn, who devoured the information, especially facts—most especially facts that others might consider to be trivia. It was impressive to hear this cute little redheaded preschooler trying to engage adults in conversations about the distinguishing characteristics of African versus Asian elephants. I emphasize the word *adults* because most children would subject themselves to a lecture on elephants for only a minute or two. Frequently, as they walked away seeking interaction that was not totally one-sided, Shawn's lack of eye contact and total absorption in his topic kept him from noticing that his audience had abandoned him, and he continued his lecture until he needed a change of pace. Adults, however, would be amazed and intrigued by a child who spoke like a little professor and would be more willing to listen for an extended period of time.

Several relatives who had been his previous "lecture attendees" gave Shawn elephant ornaments for our Christmas tree, unknowingly beginning the process of memorializing Shawn's fixations for years to come.

After a fleeting obsession with cement mixers—I still feel a rush of excitement whenever one drives by—rodents became the topic of the day. I mean week. Or in actuality several months. A collection of chipmunk, mice, and squirrel ornaments adorn our tree every year. Although no one was able to locate a guinea pig ornament, the other rodent figures always remind me of my years of constantly changing the cages of Shawn's beloved pet guinea pigs. I remember following the veterinarian's directions on how to give physical therapy to a guinea pig named Cindy, whom poor Shawn had accidentally dropped, causing her to lose the ability to move her back legs. Fortunately she never lost sensation, just her proprioception (in this case, being able to sense the positioning of her own legs; until her proprioception returned, her legs just dragged behind her, and she could not use them correctly). The proprioception in her hind legs gradually returned during the three months of my giving her daily therapy sessions.

But back at our initial appointment, when the veterinarian started to explain proprioception to Shawn and me, we were able to finish all of her sentences for her because Shawn's occupational therapist was always working on improving his general proprioception, so he could start walking through the grocery store and other places without bumping into almost everyone. Seeing Cindy the guinea pig walk normally again was a proud moment in the Lyons household, giving us hope that proprioception issues could indeed be corrected, or at least significantly improved.

Years after my days as a guinea pig's physical therapist, Shawn's connection with certain animals resurfaced in another, even more powerful fixation that brought about a surge of Christmas ornaments of a different animal motif. More on that later.

The longest-running Asperger's fixation arrived when Shawn was five, and it is still living with us now that he is a teenager. I once read him a beautifully illustrated children's book about plants, which contained a two-page spread featuring carnivorous plants. The only one I had heard of at that time was the Venus flytrap. Therefore I could not answer any of Shawn's questions about the other unusual plants in the illustration.

For him, my answering any of his questions with "I don't know" was totally unacceptable. I hated having to give this dreaded answer, because it meant he would respond by assaulting me, rapid-fire machine-gun-style, with the same question, slightly reworded each time, for an extended period.

Saying "I don't know" was like becoming the cartoon character, skiing in the Alps, whose loud sneeze triggers an enormous avalanche that sweeps down the mountainside and engulfs him in deep drifts of snow. My only hope was that the St. Bernard dogs wouldn't take too long to arrive, and that they would have something in those little kegs attached to their collars that put me out of my misery.

Library visits and gifts of informative books on Shawn's favorite topics became a lifeline for me. "If you can't beat 'em, join 'em" became a way of life for our family. Especially after a wonderful woman named Marian Joiner showed me how to not only help my son but also enjoy him.

Being Shawn's mom meant constantly careening between being astounded by his giftedness and extremely worried by his challenges and differences. A thousand such moments each day felt like an impossible balancing act. I spent so much time and energy teetering between encouraging his amazing quest for knowledge regarding his fixations and figuring out how and when to try to help him stop the cycles of repetitive monologue and questions (perseverations) that jangled my nerves and alienated other children.

I drove Shawn and his little brother, Riley, an hour each way to the church where Marian held her "Cool Kids' Club," a play group that assisted with development of social skills, and her summer day camp programs for kids in the autism spectrum. Marian always welcomed me into whatever room or outdoor space the kids were using at the time. Somehow, she was able to keep the kids engaged while simultaneously explaining or demonstrating to me the hows and whys of her therapeutic activities and the techniques she used for encouraging and shaping appropriate behavior and joyful participation.

I remember watching her push Shawn on a swing on a beautiful summer day. He was around five or six years old. He seized the moment to begin educating Marian on something very important to him: how terrestrial and aquatic Utricularia ensnare their prey in bladderlike traps. (Utricularia, in case you didn't know or guess, are a type of carnivorous plant.) To any bystander to this scenario, I was just a mom casually observing her son and his teacher. But inside I was on red alert, just dying to see how Marian would respond to what I knew could easily become one of Shawn's hour-long lectures.

Marian listened attentively for a few minutes, asking Shawn questions and praising him for his amazing display of knowledge. Suddenly, she opened her mouth and raised her arms in the most dramatic yawn I had ever seen. Shawn did not appear to notice, and continued to describe in great detail the deadly capabilities and dainty flowers of Utricularia gibba. Marian yawned again, even more dramatically and very, very loudly. When she saw that Shawn had noticed, and that he had actually come up for air between sentences, she began to state her thoughts aloud using lots of hand gestures and tons of vocal inflection, saying something like this:

> Shawn, I love hearing how much you love carnivorous plants, but my brain just can't hold all the carnivorous plant information that yours holds. It's probably because I'm interested in different things than the things that interest you, so after a while carnivorous plants become boring for me. Sooooooooooo booooooooooring! Innnnnnnnnnnncredibly boring! When people are bored, they sometimes yawn, or look away like this, or roll their eyes like this, or tap their fingers like this, or start to back away like this. Plus we're out on the playground with all the other kids, and it's time to play. Which friends out here would you like to play with right now?

Shawn was absolutely enthralled! Marian knew that for Shawn's particular sensory system high drama, enormous happy affect, and a big voice were often required to grab and maintain his attention. Plus she had him on a swing, a place where he was a captive audience and was both calm and alert because his vestibular system was receiving the extra stimulation that he required. He was not upset about having his carnivorous plant lecture interrupted. How could he be, when Marian was being so funny and interesting?

Marian had my answer. I could feed Shawn's insatiable thirst for knowledge about his favorite topics and celebrate his ability to memorize and explain his favorite facts. I could also make efforts to stop Shawn's perseverative regurgitation of his favorite facts in a way that did not squelch or reprimand him. It would actually be fun to teach Shawn appropriate social skills in a way that intrigued him and did not belittle him.

I could find a balance between promoting Shawn's giftedness and meeting the special needs he exhibited in the realm of social interaction. Marian had just demonstrated how I would be able to enjoy my son while finding the balance that would benefit him the most.

Yes, I admit it. Someone had to show me how to enjoy my son.

Shawn's fixations did much more than decorate our Christmas trees through the years. They took us to places we had never been before, on adventures that we could never have imagined.

When the International Carnivorous Plant Society decided to hold its annual international conference at the Atlanta Botanical Gardens, Shawn and I were there. Just before we walked into the place, I remember telling seven-year-old Shawn, "Honey, when we walk through these doors you are going to see an entire room full of people perseverating on the topic of carnivorous plants. It's perfectly OK to perseverate on carnivorous plants here. The people here have come from all over the world just to be able to perseverate on carnivorous plants together. Their perseverations might just result in some amazing scientific understandings and discoveries! Shawn, you go in there and enjoy every moment!"

As I followed Shawn around throughout the conference, much of the conversations and presentations were way over my head, but Shawn was having the time of his life.

There is a story in the New Testament where Mary and Joseph lose track of twelve-year-old Jesus as they are returning home from a visit to Jerusalem. They realize that Jesus must have stayed behind in Jerusalem, so in what must have been a state of enormous anxiety and panic they hurry back to Jerusalem, praying that they'll be able to find their son in such a big city. They find him in the Temple having deep, serious, challenging, theological discussions with the most learned scholars.

This Bible story jumped into my mind during lunch at the carnivorous plant conference. I must have been talking with someone as Shawn and I went to sit down with our food. When I turned around to approach the table that Shawn and I had been heading toward, I found that all the seats were taken. Shawn was sitting there eating his lunch, conversing with a table full of carnivorous plant experts, all grown men, who were speaking with him as if he were an adult. Shawn would ask a question or bring up some information he had read in one of his academic books about carnivorous plants, and then the entire group would enter into a very serious discussion. Shawn obviously understood everything they said, and his comments were a welcomed contribution to the discourse.

Jesus in the Temple and Shawn at the Conference of the International Carnivorous Plant Society. We're a Catholic family, so from time to time I find myself saying the Rosary with a group at my church. If we happen to be praying the Joyful Mysteries of the Rosary, recounting some of the happy events in the life of Christ, the fifth mystery, the Finding of the Child Jesus in the Temple, always makes me smile. In moments like this I can't help but thank God for how Shawn and his Asperger's Syndrome have enriched my life.

Between the ages of eight and eleven, along with his beloved carnivorous plants Shawn would appear as a contestant on a Nickelodeon game show called *Figure It Out* (Shawn wrote to the show about his hobby and was asked to be on it), followed by two appearances on *The Tonight Show with Jay Leno* (a producer on *Figure It Out* recommended Shawn to a friend who worked on *The Tonight Show*).

This really helped us drive home an important lesson for Shawn and our whole family: Asperger's Syndrome brings some very difficult challenges, but it also brings wonderful gifts.

There are times when perseveration and fixations can be a big stumbling block in one's social life, but they can also be a pathway to friendships, success, important discoveries, and hopefully an array of fulfilling careers from which to choose.

Meltdowns

When Shawn was five years old, he began having autism meltdowns (excruciating tantrums). This has been the most problematic and frightening aspect of his Asperger's Syndrome. Not everyone with Asperger's has meltdowns, but for those who do and for their families and teachers they can be an extremely daunting obstacle that causes enormous stress.

Shawn's meltdowns were triggered during times when he faced what to him was a major disappointment. My teacher training in early childhood education taught me that when dealing with tantrums one of the most important things was to enforce that the child should not get whatever he or she was throwing a tantrum about. The child should also receive as little attention as possible; this way the child would learn that tantrums do not work. Using standard tantrum techniques with Shawn, however, made meltdowns more frequent, and much worse.

Teaching him how to solve problems and calmly negotiate helped prevent meltdowns, but not every meltdown could be prevented. I learned that during these difficult and often very loud times Shawn primarily needed to be kept safe and repeatedly reassured that the horrible feelings he was experiencing would eventually go away. Once a meltdown started, it would continue until it burned itself out, in about thirty to forty-five minutes.

Meltdowns took various forms over the years. They could involve screaming, hitting, kicking, punching, biting, running, pushing over heavy furniture, throwing and breaking things, and even tree climbing. Tree-climbing meltdowns made me feel completely helpless, as I watched Shawn climb higher and higher, screaming and yelling all the way. Once the meltdown burned out, he would eventually climb down.

After a meltdown, Shawn would be extremely remorseful, apologetic, and confused about why the situation that precipitated the meltdown caused him to feel so desperate. Each meltdown would chip away at his self-esteem.

Thankfully, they rarely occurred at school. Shawn's facilitator and I taught all his teachers about his meltdowns, how to try to prevent them, and what to do when one started. Only once did a teacher have to follow our plan of evacuating Shawn's classmates from the classroom, fire-drill-style, so his facilitator could help keep him safe. Afterward, Shawn insisted on apologizing to his class.

A doctor once told me that because the tantrums usually occurred after school, I was obviously not doing as good a job as Shawn's teachers were at managing his behavior. The comment was quite a slap in the face, but thankfully I learned from attending lots of autism conferences, reading countless books on autism, and networking with many parents of kids with autism, that having tantrums primarily at home is a common phenomenon.

Shawn worked so hard at holding himself together at school that when he came home any disappointment or stress would cause him to fall apart.

Another doctor, whose son has severe autism, told me that kids with Asperger's Syndrome who have meltdowns are just "mean and manipulative"—words that absolutely do not describe Shawn.

I've never seen a child so driven to help others and do the right thing. Whenever Shawn thinks about using manipulation to get his way, he usually tells me that he is thinking of doing so, which obviously defeats the purpose.

To help him manage his meltdowns, we tried many behavioral and sensory techniques. If, early on, I could convince him to climb into our sensory room swing (like a hammock suspended above from one point) or lie sandwiched between two mattresses that we kept laid out in the sensory room, sometimes we could avoid dangerous behavior.

He needed to talk and scream at me while in the net swing or between the mattresses, but at least the threat of violent behavior was reduced. One my favorite tactics to defuse a brewing meltdown was encouraging Shawn to blow up raw eggs in the microwave. It was definitely messy but could be a lot of fun.

With all the behavioral, sensory, and just-plain-off-the-wall techniques we tried, none of them helped nearly as much as antiseizure medication. I did not want to give my child a medication that required regular blood draws every six months to make sure it was not harming his liver, but Shawn's psychiatrist explained that his meltdowns might be "carving problematic pathways" into the wiring in his brain, pathways that could possibly become more permanent with each meltdown, solidifying the response to stress and disappointment.

As I understood it, metaphorically, during a meltdown a sudden drop in mood caused by disappointment was causing neurons to fire like Fourth of July sparklers, sending surges of electrical activity in many directions at once, primarily in the limbic or "emotional center" of his brain. Electrical activity that was supposed to flow in a more organized circuit would run amok when triggered by a sudden mood drop. This type of chaotic electrical activity could be similar to what happens in the type of seizure that causes the body to convulse, except that these seizures affect the motor activity centers and other parts of the brain. Antiseizure medication might help to act like a surge protector of sorts for Shawn.

After starting the antiseizure medication, whenever Shawn became upset he began to say things like, "I'm really, really frustrated, but I don't feel like I need to hit anyone or break anything." This gives me a lot more hope for his future. (Note that medication that works for one child may not work at all for another, and it might even be harmful for some children. This type of medication happens to work for Shawn.)

Shawn's psychiatrist also became my psychiatrist. He understands me, because he understands my son. Antidepressant medication has helped me a great deal, although I had to try several antidepressants before finding one that works for me. Seeing a therapist to talk things through has been a lifeline for me. It took a while to find a therapist. Mine is a social worker and a good match for me. (A psychologist once told me that finding a good therapist is like going shopping for a bra. Women understand this, because after trying on several brands and styles of bras, all in the supposedly correct size, only one will actually fit.) Finding a therapist who is a good fit for me has definitely been worth the search.

The Power of Music

Way back when Shawn was between one and two years old, I noticed he was humming unusual little melodies as he went about his unique, Shawn-style of play: lining, stacking, and making elaborate sculptures with parts and pieces of his toys. Back then, I swung wildly between being impressed with his abilities and creativity to being extremely worried about how unusual he was compared to other children his age.

I was definitely impressed when I finally realized that the little melodies Shawn was humming were actually the incidental, background music from a Beatrix Potter video he loved to watch. These were not catchy tunes, but rather the stream-of-consciousness kind of music that helps paint the mood of the story, whether the characters are running or walking, anxious or peaceful, crotchety or youthful. I don't think I could hum those assortments of notes if I tried, even though I grew up singing in several choirs and dabbling in playing flute, piccolo, oboe, piano, and tuba. I remember being amazed that the fairly complex background music was what he connected with most in the cute little stories about Peter Rabbit, Jemima Puddle Duck,

Flopsy, Mopsy, and Cottontail. I remember thinking, "Wow, music really reaches my little boy."

Then there was the time I was rehearsing Schubert's "Ave Maria" in our living room. I was frequently hired as a vocalist for weddings at our family's parish church. While I was singing, the doorbell rang, smack dab in the middle of a phrase in the music. As I stopped singing to answer the door, I suddenly heard Shawn's sweet little toddler voice finish the phrase for me. He had the melody, the rhythm, and the Latin text down cold. I was astonished! After I finished speaking with the person at the door, I scooped him up and began to sing the "Ave Maria" again. I would randomly stop singing throughout the song. No matter where I stopped, he was able to sing the next few Latin words of the song.

Before Shawn was born, I taught fourth grade, preschool, and kindergarten. Field placements in college gave me opportunities to teach preschool, kindergarten, and second grade. Whenever I taught, I loved to compose little songs for my students, as a teaching tool to help them understand tricky concepts or help with the rote memorization that is difficult for some kids. One reason I went into early childhood education was because singing, dancing, and creative drama could be part of my job. These were the hobbies that had brought me so much enjoyment from childhood through adulthood. It's perfectly acceptable for a teacher to burst into song in the middle of her workday, and there aren't too many careers out there for which this is true. It's also perfectly acceptable for a mom to do a lot of singing with her young children; it was just part of how I functioned as a parent. I sang a lot with Shawn because he loved it. I wrote several little songs for the two of us. We had a nursing song, a diaper-changing song, and lots of songs for things we did throughout our day.

When Shawn started to babble and speak as an infant (his language developed very early, with an extremely brief babbling stage that quickly was replaced by words), I would pay attention to what sounds or words he repeated and then wrack my brain for any catchy songs I knew that contained the particular word or sound. At the time, we lived in a brand new house for which we had selected and purchased all the landscaping plants. When I took Shawn outside to toddle around the yard, I would tell him the names of the plants he approached (at least the names I could remember).

Some of his favorite bushes were called "taxis." He loved saying the word "taxis" and would repeat it over and over. I began singing to Shawn, "The stars at night are big and bright, bum, bum, bum, bum, deep in the heart of Texas. . . . " After singing it a few times through, I began stopping just before that word which recurs at the end of several phrases in the song. He would jump right in, finishing the phrases by singing the word "taxis." It was very goofy and silly and made no sense, but Shawn absolutely loved it. He had always been a baby who was unusually content with being by himself and keeping himself occupied, so singing songs together in this fashion gave us a way to connect. In a way, the singing back and forth with Shawn was almost conversational.

In the years following Shawn's Asperger's Syndrome diagnosis (which occurred at three years, eleven months), I would learn that the technique of leaving off the last word in a phrase of a song is one that music therapists use in teaching children with language delay how to talk. The child's need to hear a musical chord resolve itself at the end of a musical phrase can almost seem to pull the words out of a child who struggles to speak. If you don't believe me, or don't understand what I am referring to, try singing "Row, Row, Row Your Boat" while leaving off the last word in the song. You will feel compelled to resolve the chord by finishing the song.

Shawn's love of and attention to singing led me to sing directions to him if he was spaced out and not seeming to hear my requests. I would improvise my own weird little melodies for telling him to put on his shoes, clean up some toys, or walk with his heels striking first instead of his usual tippy-toe walking. I found that for him sung directions were much more effective than spoken ones, no matter how strange the melody or whether the words rhymed as they do in most children's songs.

Songs could also be used to help him understand that we were getting ready to finish one activity and begin something new. This helped him cope with transitions, which could be very difficult for him. I made up an extremely goofy song that I always sang when placing him on the toilet during his potty training. It helped him to measure time, because when the song was done he could ask to get down, or he would understand to stay put when I told him (or sang to him) that we were going to sing the song again. Of course, I didn't sing all the time throughout our days, but singing was a helpful trick to have up my sleeve whenever he was struggling or unable to focus.

As potty training continued, Shawn struggled to complete the many steps that follow the actual using of the toilet: flushing, pulling pants up, and so on. Water running over Shawn's hands in the sink would completely mesmerize him, keeping him from proceeding to the steps of soaping up, rinsing, turning off the water, and drying his hands. I wrote a song that took him through all the steps. When I sang it, he would follow all the steps in correct order and wouldn't get stuck on any one step. During the months after Riley was born (the boys are almost exactly three years apart), my attending to Riley meant that Shawn would sometimes be in the bathroom for a few minutes without me. If I heard him proclaiming that he had just used the toilet, I would call out to him, "Sing your 'I Can Use the Bathroom by Myself' song!" It was so funny to hear him down the hallway, singing the whole song with his usual gusto. He began to make it through all the steps in order, without me.

It's important to mention that Shawn seemed to be completely oblivious to the presence of his new baby brother in our house. If it weren't for the fact that Shawn was impressed by Riley's propensity for projectile vomiting, it was almost as if he weren't there. As a toddler, Riley was diagnosed with severe regulatory disorder (a term from Dr. Stanley Greenspan), sensory integration dysfunction, and a mild language delay. I have noticed that many siblings of kids in the autism spectrum have what I like to call a few little "pieces of autism," such as Riley's diagnoses, attention deficit, learning disabilities, obsessive-compulsive disorder, and others. Because of what Shawn had taught us, we knew to have Riley evaluated by many of the same therapists and doctors that worked with Shawn. If it were not for Shawn, we would have just thought that Riley was an extremely fussy, difficult baby and toddler. It's odd to think back on, but regretfully, I didn't do nearly as much singing with Riley as I had with Shawn during his very early years. Perhaps it was because Riley was so unhappy most of the time and didn't respond to music the way Shawn did.

I also suspect that I was experiencing some postpartum depression. We began Riley's early intervention therapies starting around eighteen months, and we saw much more rapid progress with Riley than we had with Shawn.

In his early school years, Riley had some mild behavioral struggles that were caused by his neurological glitches, but these struggles ended by third grade. Today, very few people would suspect that Riley had any neurological glitches at all. His sensory differences regarding his proprioceptive system (Riley thrives on bash-and-crash sports activities) have translated into his becoming an awesome soccer goalie. Riley is also a caring friend to his peers and has a great sense of humor. Despite the many challenges that Riley has faced and continues to deal with as the brother of a kid with Asperger's Syndrome, Riley goes out of his way to spot classmates who have problems with social skills and try to help them. His compassion far exceeds that of a typical fourteen-year-old boy.

I began to write story songs that illustrated some of Shawn's struggles with social skills. I tried to make the songs funny and playful, full of suggestions on how to follow the social rules of neurotypical society whenever life made this necessary. For example, a song called "It's OK to Play Differently" (the "Arranging Song") described Shawn's style of playing, which caused him more than a little grief with his classmates in preschool and early elementary grades. The song explains that when playing with other kids, it is important to them to be able to share their own ideas. The song describes Shawn's anger when classmates, who gathered around whenever he built block structures, tried to add blocks that were not part of Shawn's well-planned designs. The song's story concludes with Shawn becoming flexible enough to allow classmates to place blocks where they would like to in his block structures at school, knowing that whenever he played alone at home he could arrange his own blocks and toys just the way he wanted them to be, to his heart's content.

Another song that helped Shawn a great deal was "Perseveration Station," which tells the story of a train that gets stuck in the station and is unable to move on. The song describes how people feel when someone gets stuck on one conversation topic and will not move on. It also explains that if someone catches himself or herself perseverating, it is helpful to stop and ask one's conversation partner what he or she likes to do, giving the other person a chance to contribute to the conversation.

Back when I was writing my first social skill songs, I had not yet learned how to play the guitar. Mike Meehan, a friend from church choir, came up with guitar accompaniments to the songs that I sang a cappella into a tape recorder. Mike and I performed the songs for a few autism support groups in our area. Parents kept telling me that their children needed my songs, so thanks to the support of my husband and my parents I had my songs professionally arranged, accompanied, and recorded on a CD that I called *Gather Stars for Your Children: Songs to Enhance Social Skills and Foster a Welcoming Attitude.*

In the following year, 1998, someone at *Dateline NBC* read an article, which appeared in the newspaper where we live in metro Atlanta, describing my music and how it helped Shawn. *Dateline* arranged for a camera crew to follow my family around, videotaping footage for two days and editing it down to be part of a short segment about how music can be used to help kids with autism. I could never make a living out of writing and recording my songs, but I tell people who ask about it that I'm definitely in the "autism top forty." Sales of my first CD made enough money for me to finance the musical arrangements and recording time for my second CD. It is taking me a very long time to finish the second CD, which I seem to be able to do only one baby step at a time. I know it will happen, but it will have to happen in God's time.

Back when *Dateline NBC* spent those two days following us around, trying to capture moments in which my singing to nine-year-old Shawn made his life easier, something heart-wrenching happened. After the first day of filming, the NBC crew told me that Shawn appeared incredibly "normal," perhaps too normal to effectively illustrate Asperger's Syndrome for their viewing audience.

At bedtime that night, Shawn told me, with his usual level of complete honesty, "Mom, I was trying so hard today. I don't think I let them see even a tiny bit of my autism features." On the second day of filming, the intense level of concentration and superhuman effort that Shawn had expended the day before, trying to appear completely normal, all caught up with him. I unwittingly sabotaged my son that day by taking him to the post office and making him wait while I put together and addressed a package or two of my CDs, the orders for which had just arrived in my P.O. box. Waiting was always difficult for Shawn. I didn't realize that the waiting coupled with his having burned himself out the day before in trying so hard to hide his autism features would launch him into one of his autism meltdowns. The film crew caught the entire meltdown on tape, right there on the post office floor, which is where Shawn and I ended up. They talked with Shawn afterward, once his meltdown burned itself out. They said they would use that footage only if he gave them his permission.

I felt incredible guilt for putting my son in such a difficult situation. That night at bedtime, I read to him from a book by Jane Taylor McDonnell titled *News from the Border*. It is a wonderful memoir written by the mom of a son with autism. The Afterword chapter at the end of the book is written by her son, Paul, who as a young man wrote his own side of his story, including some descriptions of his own autism meltdowns and other embarrassing moments. That night I read Paul's words to Shawn and asked how it felt for him to be able to read that someone else with autism spectrum differences experienced bad meltdowns too. Shawn was fascinated by Paul's honest descriptions of his problems and said they made him feel better. I told Shawn that if he decided to let *Dateline NBC* use the meltdown footage there was a chance that showing it on TV would help other people who had autism meltdowns to feel a little better, to see that they were not the only ones who experienced such terrible and frightening episodes in their lives. I told Shawn that the footage might help people who would see it on TV to better understand people with autism spectrum differences. I knew that I was asking a lot of my little boy, and I was feeling horribly guilty about it, wondering if it was right to lay this big decision on him. After a while, Shawn told me that he wanted to do what Paul had done. Shawn gave permission for his meltdown to be shown on national TV. About six months later, the story aired. Rory and I thought it did a good job showing how worthwhile it is to try using music in different ways as a possibility for helping people throughout the autism spectrum.

We received some interesting letters in our P.O. box following the airing of that segment. One letter, from a mom, said that seeing Shawn on TV (especially the meltdown footage) helped her parents to believe in her son's diagnosis of Asperger's Syndrome for the first time. They finally stopped accusing her of being a bad parent and were beginning to be supportive of her and her son instead of offering nothing but criticism. I read the letter to Shawn, explaining that his difficult decision had helped a child in the spectrum to finally be loved and accepted by his grandparents.

School

Rory and I have always placed Shawn in regular education classrooms so he could be surrounded by peers who exhibited typical social interaction. His particular sensory challenges allowed him to handle this fairly well. For children with Asperger's Syndrome who have extreme hearing sensitivities, or extreme sensory defensiveness related to touch or visual stimulation, this type of placement might not work. Shawn's greatest sensory challenges stem from a vestibular system that craves lots of extra input.

He required opportunities throughout the school day, to give the fluid in the semicircular canal of his inner ear a chance to do some major sloshing around. We learned about this through occupational therapy that emphasized sensory integration. As long as Shawn had access to equipment on which he could spin himself very rapidly for several minutes at a time, several times a day, and a chance to do some other well-chosen gross motor exercises, he could function pretty comfortably in a regular classroom. (It is extremely important to consult with an occupational therapist with expertise in sensory integration before trying spinning activities with a child. For some children, spinning can be harmful if not done correctly.)

We knew that just being surrounded by typically developing peers was not enough for Shawn. To learn how to participate in neurotypical social interaction, he also required the assistance of an interpreter who could explain the facial expressions, body language, tone of voice, figurative language, and feelings of his classmates in a variety of situations as they occurred in his classrooms. We called these interpreters "facilitators." Shawn required the assistance of a highly trained facilitator from preschool through the first semester of high school.

Our public school system would not provide a facilitator, let alone one with training in autism spectrum disorders, for Shawn because his academic skills were phenomenal. We did not want to waste the time, blood, sweat, and tears that it would take to fight the school system, so we found a small church-affiliated school that would accept Shawn and allow him to come to school with a facilitator whom we would train and whose position we would fund. This was a costly endeavor that we realize is not an option for most families, but fortunately Rory's job afforded us the ability to attempt it.

I felt fairly comfortable designing and supervising Shawn's inclusion program because of my training in early childhood education, and because all of Shawn's therapists and doctors (speech and language pathologists, occupational therapists specializing in sensory integration, physical therapists, psychologists, psychiatrists, music therapists, and social skills group leaders) had been willing to let me observe their work with Shawn and explain the techniques they used. We even had some of them observe Shawn at school, during his kindergarten year, so they could see him with his classmates and make suggestions that his facilitator and I could follow.

With autism spectrum disorders, every family situation is unique. Family finances; the temperament and background of parents and other family members; the availability of state Medicaid deeming waivers to pay for the therapies, doctors visits, and medications; the support of extended family members; as well as each child's completely unique needs and gifts mean that the family has to follow its own path, whether it involves public school, home schooling, full inclusion, partial inclusion, use of facilitators or one-on-one paraprofessionals, pursuing litigation or mediation with a public school system that will not meet a child's needs, private schools, special education schools, self-contained special education classrooms . . . the list goes on and on.

Shawn's facilitators have had an absolutely huge impact on his life, helping him day by day to learn the intricate details of neurotypical social interaction, to try to see the similarities and differences in each interaction so he can memorize the information, generalize it to other situations, and apply what he has learned to brand-new situations. They tried to do all of this in a way that let Shawn know his ways of playing and conversing were not wrong, just different, and by learning how to successfully interact in neurotypical culture he would have many more opportunities and choices in life.

Shawn had two long-term facilitators over the years. Kathy Schreiner was his teacher in a private, inclusive preschool when we first moved to Atlanta. Several of the special needs preschool students there had facilitators. As Shawn was finishing his last year of preschool, she approached us saying that if we ever wanted to hire a facilitator for him she would love to apply for the position. She was a gift from heaven. In the small church school Shawn attended from kindergarten through third grade, she diligently and lovingly coached him on social interaction skills and helped him learn to begin to recognize and meet his own sensory needs. The school let us set up Shawn's two spin boards in a little alcove down the hall from his classrooms, and Kathy would accompany him there when he needed to spin for a few minutes. Sometimes she would take him outside to swing on the playground, as another way to give his inner ear fluid a good slosh. Kathy kept a detailed journal of how Shawn was doing each day, so I could read it and we could identify ways to help Shawn succeed.

Kathy and I provided training in Shawn's version of Asperger's Syndrome to his teachers and his classmates. I found that my songs about social skills and autism spectrum differences were fun to use as part of autism awareness presentations for Shawn's classmates. The students learned the songs and would even sing them to him during times when he needed the reminders in the songs. I remember coming to volunteer in Shawn's class one day, stepping into the room and discovering six-year-old Hillary singing my "Personal Space Invader" song to Shawn, who had forgotten that standing eyeball to eyeball can be uncomfortable for neurotypical kids.

Shawn's school housed grades preschool through five, so we began to worry about eventually having to send him to a middle school, which would be a huge change coinciding with the difficult changes every child faces during puberty. Fortunately, a brand-new Catholic school for grades kindergarten through eight opened within a few minutes' drive of our house, and we are Catholic. The principal, Sister Patricia Clune, accepted Shawn into the school's fourth grade class, even though the competition for spaces at the school was fierce. Sister Patricia said she wanted many kinds of diversity at Queen of Angels Catholic School, and she thought Shawn and his facilitator would be a wonderful addition. God bless her for taking a chance on us. Kathy Schreiner was a certified teacher and was hired by Shawn's previous school to be a classroom teacher, so we had to find a new facilitator for him.

Through the mighty network of parents of kids with autism spectrum differences, I found Cindy Hart. She was finishing up work as a facilitator for another child and was looking for a new position. Through families she had worked for previously, she received on-the-job training and was certified as a "floor time" practitioner. "Floor time," developed by Dr. Greenspan, was a wonderful fit for Shawn's preferred ways of learning social interaction skills. Cindy, like Kathy, knew that hovering over him in his classroom would not be helpful, because it would promote dependence. Kathy and Cindy were great about circulating throughout the classroom, helping any student who asked, but always keeping a watchful eye on Shawn and being ready to intervene at any teachable moment, in playful ways that conveyed their deep respect for him. Schools often tell parents that seeking a paraprofessional or facilitator for their child can be harmful, because the child becomes dependent on the person. This is not true if the facilitator is properly trained and knows how to work in ways that foster independence. If Shawn were able to learn typical social interaction skills without having a facilitator there to interpret, teach, and coach him, he wouldn't have Asperger's Syndrome.

As Shawn became increasingly independent, capable of recognizing and meeting his own sensory needs, and socially adept, and as he developed mutually enjoyable friendships, Cindy found creative ways to phase herself out. She began helping other kids, elsewhere in the building, though wearing a pager on her belt. Shawn was allowed to have access to the telephone in a nearby teacher workroom. Whenever he noticed that he was becoming too slumpy or too wound-up to pay attention (even while sitting on an exercise ball at his desk, instead of using a chair), he would get permission from his teacher to leave the classroom and call Cindy's pager from the workroom phone; she would arrive in a few minutes to accompany him to his sensory room. Teachers sometimes worried that Shawn would take advantage of this set up just to get out of class, but he inevitably told Cindy if he was just being manipulative and she would help him make better choices. The honesty of Asperger's Syndrome is refreshing.

Other students were allowed to use Shawn's sensory materials if they needed them and did so appropriately. A few of Shawn's classmates found they could pay attention better in class if they sat on his exercise ball for a few minutes, in place of a chair. During tests, several students began to come to Cindy to borrow Shawn's stress balls and other hand-fidget materials, finding they could use them to alleviate stress and concentrate better during their tests. Cindy and I talked on the phone whenever necessary, sometimes several times per week, to brainstorm and strategize ways to best help Shawn with his behavior, social skills, friendship development, sensory issues, organizational skills, and any tricky situations that might arise.

In spite of all our efforts, his middle school years were extra challenging. There were many kids in class who maintained a kind, respectful, and friendly attitude toward him, but they were unable to resist the efforts of one boy who became an "alpha male" in Shawn's class during his middle school years. This boy, who developed athletic prowess and had an impressive growth spurt, seemed to make it his life's mission to belittle and harass Shawn. He was also quite a con artist with the school's new administration and with his parents. Cindy and I realized that this boy needed serious help, but there was little we could do.

Shawn needed to take more sensory room breaks during the school days of his middle school years, which made it difficult sometimes to stay on top of his various school subjects and keep himself organized. He and Cindy and I muddled through his middle school years the best we could. She provided enormous support for Shawn. As he spun on one of the spin boards in his sensory area, she would help him talk through the difficulties he experienced in dealing with the seismically shifting social rules of adolescence. Shawn was amazed that if he spoke to a girl in the hallway one week some of his classmates would tease him mercilessly, and the very next week it was actually cool to talk with a girl between classes.

Physical education classes became frustrating too, because of the way the boys harassed one another in the locker rooms, and also because of what my husband and I refer to as the "President's Physical Fitness Humiliation Test." This test gained huge importance among Shawn's male peers during the middle school years, and it put numerical values to Shawn's struggles with muscle tone, coordination, and slightly delayed development in comparison to his classmates.

High school has been such a relief for Shawn—a thousand times better than the middle school years. Shawn goes to a public high school that has magnet programs for math, science, the performing arts, and the visual arts. This public high school was so impressed with Shawn's abilities in social skills and sensory self-regulation that they jumped at the chance to hire his facilitator, Cindy, to help him transition into such a different environment with so many more students than what he had previously experienced in school. The kids who attend this school as their local high school are from widely diverse socioeconomic, racial, and ethnic backgrounds. There is a large population of nerds walking the halls, because of the advanced math and science programs, and a comparable population of eccentric, artsy kids. It is the only high school I've ever walked into in my adult life in which I did not immediately experience an emotional time warp, suddenly, inexplicably, feeling myself being sucked back into the horribly self-conscious feelings I experienced in my own high school days.

It is OK to be who you are at Shawn's school, and he is thriving there. He has had to learn some street smarts at this school, oftentimes the hard way. However, I think it's much better for him to learn them in high school than when he's away at college. But the teachers, who are used to eccentric students and who have learned how to maintain the attention of high school students over ninety-minute blocks of time (because the school follows a block schedule of four classes per day), have worked very well with him.

This high school turned out to be such a good fit for Shawn that he no longer needed Cindy after his first semester. She worked herself out of a job. Both the special education teachers and regular education teachers still ask me about how she's doing, and they always comment on how much they learned from her. We will never be able to thank her enough for everything she did for Shawn.

Shawn has built up incredible stamina for withstanding the workload at his school, which amazes me. He no longer has spin boards in a supply closet at school, but after school he still uses the spinning tire swing that we have in our back yard. In each classroom he has an exercise ball tucked away, which he uses instead of a chair when he feels the need for additional vestibular input during classes. At the beginning of each semester, the school allows me to offer training in Shawn's version of Asperger's Syndrome for any teachers who are working with him for the first time. He participates in these training sessions now, and each semester he takes over more of the training presentation. He is learning to advocate for himself.

Cats were a major fixation for Shawn several years ago, and we have the Christmas ornaments to prove it. Because of Shawn, we have four cats in our household. His continuing interest in cats led Shawn to pursue an internship for one semester this year, working at the Cat Clinic of Roswell for one and a half hours each morning before heading to school. Working as a high school intern at the Cat Clinic was a wonderful experience for Shawn. Sure, he did a lot of litter box scooping, but he also was allowed to observe surgeries and found out that he doesn't become the least bit queasy during surgical procedures—not even in the amputation of the leg of one of his favorite kittens there. Each school day, as I drove Shawn from the Cat Clinic to school, he would tell me all about the social situations the cats up for adoption would get into among themselves as they roamed about the clinic. It was like listening to a cat soap opera. I truly believe that his observations of cats have helped him learn to be more observant of social interactions among humans and learn independently through these observations, particularly with regard to body language, which is a feline's main method of communication.

One morning Shawn told me that beginning each school day morning with his work at the Cat Clinic made the rest of the day go better. My theory is that his Cat Clinic work was an ideal match for his sensory requirements. His work required him to move around a lot, doing some heavy lifting, and he had the opportunity to handle several cats each day. I've explained to Shawn that it will be important for him to go into a career that is a good match for his sensory system.

He says that in college he would like to study botany or other plant sciences, but perhaps he would consider veterinary school as a fallback position. Go, Shawn!

8

THE FREEDOM
TO BE ODD

[BY CAMMIE McGOVERN]

(Cammie McGovern is a novelist, ASD activist, and mother of three. Her oldest child, Ethan, carries a diagnosis in the autism spectrum. His "difficulties" have inspired a novel and the founding of a resource center called Whole Children, which runs after-school classes and programs for children with special needs. —RP)

For every parent of a child in the autism spectrum, there is a familiar dilemma: the child needs help learning to socialize and navigate what is, for him, the Byzantine world of ordinary children playing ordinary games at recess. Yet how do you do it? How do you ask thirty-five children running around a playground to stop what they're doing, explain a game of tag, and start again—slowly, without too much noise, so this one "different" boy can join and finally learn a concept that eludes him so mysteriously ("Tag! You're it!")?

The answer, of course, is you can't. Even in a school that has been mainstreaming children with special needs steadily and successfully for almost twenty years, where the general population of children are blissfully accustomed to wheelchairs, walkers, and sign language interpreters, autism presents its own special challenge.

These kids may look normal, but for most of them the art of play with other children is monumentally complicated. For one thing, children's play often takes place in chaotic settings, outside, where there are lawnmowers and airplanes to grab their attention and pull it away.

There are also extraneous conversations, the distraction of laughter and crying, all of it impossible for an ASD child to block out. Not all play requires talking, but some of it certainly does. There are rules to establish, and some back-and-forth to negotiate. For children to whom language has come late and remains a perpetual stumbling block, the quick chatter on the playground (or anywhere else for that matter) is often impossible to keep up with.

Where do you go to learn these basics? How do you tell a joke? Suggest a game? Ask other children what they are playing and if you can join?

Three years ago, a group of six other parents and I (primarily mothers) started a center called Whole Children to run after-school classes for children with special needs. At the time, it was a lark. We'd met in a summer gymnastics class, and we liked one another and the relief of being with other mothers who shared the same issues. We wanted to make the gymnastics program year-round with its own site, full of the sensory equipment these children crave and often need: swings, trampolines, parallel bars, balance boards, a ball pit.

Truthfully, I joined the effort as much for myself as anything else. Having a child with special needs can be isolating in a way that is hard to describe to anyone except another parent who knows all too well. At the time, I actually thought we wouldn't use the center all that much.

My son Ethan is reasonably coordinated. Though the program certainly couldn't hurt, I presumed that his most acute needs would not be addressed by a gymnastics class.

Then, on his first day at the new center, I watched Ethan crawl along the ground to keep an eye on a girl he'd just met who had cerebral palsy (CP). Though she could walk unsteadily on her own, she walked better holding a hand. For a while, her mother stayed by her side; then, about halfway through, Ethan surprised everyone by stepping over to the girl and offering his hand. They stayed together for the rest of the class, as her mother and I watched from the sidelines.

Toward the end of the session, her mother shook her head: "She's trying to keep up with him. He's getting her to do things I probably couldn't." The passing remark took my breath away. We had spent Ethan's whole life emphasizing the importance of being with "typical" kids, using them as models, prompting him through play dates and games he never enjoyed much or saw the point of doing.

Finally, it occurred to me: When had Ethan ever been better than another child at anything? When had he experienced the joy that comes from helping someone else?

Since we began our Whole Children effort, what I have seen continues to surprise me. Ethan seems to recognize intuitively what he shares with these children, and in their presence he relaxes more. Just as the children with CP arrive at the center, slide out of their braces, and leave their walkers at the door, Ethan sheds something too: the weight of conforming his body and controlling its natural impulses.

He bounces happily from one end of the room to the other. He connects with other children—not just in the ways he has been taught at school, with high fives and socially appropriate questions. He says hello by grabbing an elbow and kissing it, or by getting down on the floor and examining someone's shoe. "It's got holes!" he announces when he stands back up, as if he's never noticed before what defines a sandal. And maybe he hasn't. In the hard work of getting through his school day, when is there time to look at a girl's clothes and take in the specifics?

Of course, Ethan isn't the only child who's benefiting from Whole Children. We began offering more classes: music, art, yoga, woodworking, recess games. From a parent's perspective, all of these classes are targeting weaknesses, integrating therapy to build up skills in the guise of play.

What I see as I watch Ethan interact with other children his age who are learning to walk, balance on one foot, or hold a pencil is that he is quietly and steadily making gains on the skills that have for so long eluded him. He notices other children now, hears what they say to him, well enough now to answer about 50 percent of the time.

There is, of course, an irony to this discovery. We special-needs parents have spent more than twenty years in a battle to end segregated classrooms for our children. As the beneficiary of this fight, I can see the countless ways in which it's important for all children to have equal access to the same education. There is a world, after all, populated primarily by people without disabilities. To live in this world one day, with some measure of independence, will require a lifetime of practice that must begin when children are young.

Given this philosophy, it's counterintuitive to argue that segregated recreation is an answer. Yet, having watched how this approach works, I would say that it's certainly one answer.

For years, we tried valiantly to sign up Ethan for the same activities his typical peers were doing, but all of our efforts felt forced. Swimming lessons were a trial, beginning soccer an exercise in watching him pluck at blades of grass and retreat to a pile of sand he could sift through his fingers. We'd cajole and prompt him with ludicrous rewards: "Kick the ball once and you can go back to the sand," we'd scream from the side. He would nod, do as he was told, and return to his real pleasure.

At Whole Children, the experience has been entirely different, and looking at that difference has taught me something about the point of play. Ideally, in its truest form play should come from the child, reflect who he is and if possible be apart from adults, with all their well-intentioned direction, prodding, and prompting. If play is the beginning of measuring the world and finding one's place in it, it shouldn't be hard or embarrassing. One should feel successful.

These days I watch Ethan with his friends at Whole Children. He knows the regular crowd well enough now that he moves away from me and stands with them in the lobby, waiting for class. Today, one boy is trying to teach the others how to make an armpit fart—surely not a skill any adult would prioritize, but Ethan is fascinated, working hard to get the trick of it. When he fails after five minutes, I hear him say something entirely new for him: "Listen to this, guys." I hold my breath, trying to imagine what might follow. He then clears his throat and sings, in his beautiful perfect pitch: "Twinkle, twinkle, little poop." The whole group laughs, one boy so hard he falls on the floor.

To characterize this as a breakthrough might seem a stretch, and yet it is, in a dozen ways. Apart from having meltdowns, Ethan has never drawn attention to himself before, never told a joke to a group, never made a crowd laugh.

I can see his whole body register the thrill. He bounces over to me, repeats the joke, then bounces back to the crowd that, in all honesty, appreciated it a little more than I do.

He's standing taller, beaming at his audience. He looks different in this setting, as if now, having told a joke, anything is possible.

Anything at all.

9

JUST A LITTLE
AUTISM

[BY TERESA BECERRA]

*(Teresa Becerra is a mom, writer, lecturer, activist, and much more.
Her son, "Little Robert," has inspired her and her family to reach out and
connect with the ASD community, She and her husband, "Big Robert"
(author of the next chapter), are two of the most amazing people I have
ever met. —RP)*

Not long after the September 11 terrorist attacks, I had to take an evening
flight from Florida to Connecticut with my youngest child, four-year-old
Robert. Venturing out to the airport was definitely nerve-wracking, but not
for the expected reasons.

"Little Robert"—so nicknamed because of his "Jr." status—has an autism spectrum diagnosis. In other words, he's not always at his best in loud, crowded, and tense situations.

We got to the airport, checked in, made it through the array of new security precautions without incident, and headed down the concourse to our gate. We had to take an escalator at one point, and when we got to the bottom "Little" stepped off and immediately stood to the side. He had me stand next to him as he watched the feet of the next one hundred or so people step off the escalator. Foot after foot, Little watched intensely, mesmerized by the repetitive motion. He managed to get in a self-stimulating arm flap or two; once he was satisfied, we continued on to the gate.

I remember thinking, as we walked, "What is that fascinates him so much about watching people's feet step off an escalator? He obviously gets pleasure and satisfaction out of it, but what exactly?"

We got to the gate. I sat down. Little sat next to me. Suddenly, he decided to get up and move, so he jumped up and dashed to an empty row of uncomfortable seats. He laid down, face up, and started to scoot his butt across the smooth vinyl. As I sat and watched him, I felt a strong surge of motherly pride: "How cute is that? And how typical for a four-year-old boy."

Assured everything was going to be all right for at least the next fifteen seconds, I glanced down at our tickets. When I looked up, Little was chewing something. I raced to his side and saw that he was chomping a piece of gum he had pried from the bottom of an armrest.

I reached in Little's mouth, pulled out the nasty red saliva-soaked substance, and explained how this was not a good thing to do. Since he doesn't speak, he looked at me as though it was no big thing. It definitely wasn't the first time Little had chewed someone else's gum, and I knew it wouldn't be the last. I took it all in stride and sat back down, shaking my head and thinking, "I couldn't make this stuff up if I tried."

Fasten Your Seat Belts, We're in for a Bumpy Ride

The sun was setting as we boarded the plane. I found our seats, and we got comfortable. Little has always been a good in-flight boy. We took off.

At cruising altitude, the flight attendants appeared with snacks and drinks. Little and I ate, and we played with his special toys. He was quiet and content.

As the cabin grew darker, other passengers were turning on their overhead lights so they could read their magazines and books. I pulled out Little's portable DVD player, already loaded with his favorite movie of all time, *Toy Story*.

One by one, I could see the heads of the people in the rows in front of us start to nod off. Eventually, it appeared that most were sound asleep. I began feeling turbulence in my stomach as Little's "flapping" part of the film approached—the scene where Buzz and Woody have a heated discussion about Buzz's ability to fly.

Little's hand flaps started. Within seconds, I saw his jaw drop. I braced myself. Buzz began flying on screen. I knew what was coming next.

"Whoooooooooooooooooooopeeeeeeeeeeeeeeahhhhhhhhhhhhhhhhhhgussssssssh." Little screeched in his biggest voice.

Given the post–September 11 timing of the flight, the extreme reaction in the cabin was understandable. Every single passenger in front of us suddenly jumped up, several hitting their head on the plastic ceiling above them. There was, of course, shock and panic on most of their faces. I couldn't blame them. We were flying to the Northeast, after all. Thankfully, though, neither Little nor I fit the FBI terrorist profile.

Centering myself, I calmly rose up, red-faced, and said, "It's OK, it's OK, go back to sleep. It's just a little autism, folks. Just a little autism." As they sat back down, all looked relieved and reassured. I crashed in my seat too, as Little remained engrossed in Woody and Buzz. "It's just a little autism . . . just a little autism."

Being the mother of a child with autism is an incredible experience. I have my "I wish other moms could be with Little Robert for a day and get to experience what I do" days. No question, my son demands a lot of energy.

Children with autism—especially Little, who carries the "severe" label— do not process or act in the world the way we typicals do. For example, we see a chandelier, and we know its function is to light up a room, so we look at it and leave it alone.

Little's brain tells him to go up to it and give it a good swat so he can watch it swing. Then he likes to flap his hands like a little bird and yell at it. My brain tells me to tell him no and go over and stop it from swinging. But the truth is, there is also a part of me that enjoys watching, because it is not something one sees every day.

Another example is walking down the street with Little and coming to a curb. He cannot just cross the street without reaching down and feeling the curb, tracing it ever so gently with his pointer finger. Why is a curb so fascinating? Aren't curbs supposed to be totally taken for granted? But, when you are a mom of one of these incredible children, you have to stop too. You stand there and watch and suddenly it dawns on you that the man who made that curb had just as much appreciation for his craft as Little does.

It's in those autism moments that you realize our lives should really be about appreciating what's around us, living in the moment.

That's why, even though Little can totally drive me crazy and drain all of my energy, I am grateful for the lesson and for the child who put it in front of me.

Before Little came into our lives, I was one of those moms who always wondered what life would be like with a special child. I was blessed with two typical kids at the time. When I saw moms out with their special children, I would always think to myself, "How do they do it?"

Years ago, when my girls were young, there was a mom with three boys living across the street. Her middle son, Tommy, had a crush on Karlee, my daughter, and he would come visit from time to time. I felt for Tommy because his younger brother had cerebral palsy and was in a wheelchair. You could tell he adored his brother, which really made me admire him even more. Their mom would bring Tommy's brother over on Halloween, all dressed up in his wheelchair, and it would break my heart. I couldn't even imagine. I had so many questions for her but never found the courage to ask them. I guess I just wanted to know how she felt inside.

I realize now that she knew the gift she had too. You could tell by her face: she was at total peace with it. There are women we all admire throughout our lives, but we don't tell them, for whatever reason. She was one I wish I had told. She was truly a role model, as I hope I am for the special moms I come into contact with today.

Life-Changing Experiences

I've had many experiences in my life that led me to where I am today. My sister Laurie is convinced that I was given a second chance at life because I had more work to do. I think now she's right; I know I wasn't ready to go when I was asked. The date was January 19, 1977. I was just nineteen years old. Two tumors were discovered in one of my breasts, and I had to leave college to come back home to Miami for surgery. I was really scared because they told me if the tumors were malignant I would have to have my breast removed. I signed the papers alone the night before my surgery, and I cried myself to sleep. In the morning, my sister and my mom came to be with me.

After the surgery, I remember just barely waking up enough to tell them I felt really sick. But before they could even go get someone to help, the doctors and nurses started flooding my room. I remember them yelling out my blood pressure numbers, and I remember hearing them say, "She's coded." Suddenly, I found myself watching them working on me from above, but I didn't stay in the room too long because I was worried about my sister and my mom. I floated into the hallway to check on them, and I could see that they were worried. Then I left there and seemed to be nowhere for a while. It was very peaceful, just floating. I didn't see any light or a tunnel that I can remember, but I was asked a question that wasn't put in the form of a voice. Just an internal question, if that makes any sense.

I know I responded very quickly and said, "I don't want to go, I'm not ready yet, I want to go back and have children, I want to be a mother." To this day, I don't know how long I was gone, but I'm sure it's somewhere in my medical records. I've just never asked for them.

The strangest thing happened when I finally awoke. My mom and sister came in and started to tell me that it was snowing outside. I thought for a minute that I was still dead. How could it be snowing? We lived in Miami, and it had never snowed there. My mom went over to the window and pulled back the curtain to try to show me the light snow that was falling, but I couldn't see it. However, it was true; it did snow in Miami that morning. It's a matter of record.

Days after the surgery, I told my sister and my mom what I had experienced, but I made them both promise not to tell anyone because in

1977 no one talked about those sorts of things. I didn't want anyone to think I was a wacko, so for years I did not share my near-death experience with anyone. I was happy to share the results of the biopsy, though: thankfully, both tumors were benign.

It was a life-changing experience. Prior to that, I was a nineteen-year-old girl who only thought about herself and her appearance. I was very vain and self-absorbed. I only cared about my hair, my body, my clothes, my next night out on the town, and of course boys. After the surgery and the experience I had, I knew what was important in my life, and I knew I was changing for the better. I was given a second chance at life. It was the ultimate wake-up call.

A few years later, on February 6, 1979, I gave birth to my first daughter, Natalee. Beautiful and perfect, she was amazing to her father and me. Then the following year, on June 30, we had Karlee. Equally beautiful and wonderful, she completed our great little family. The two of them kept me busy, but I enjoyed them so much. They were funny, witty, smart, talented, lovable, and the highlight of my life. They still are to this day. I adore them, I admire them, I respect the exceptional women they've become, and I don't take them for granted at all. I know how lucky I was to be able to raise them and enjoy all the normal experiences a mom should have.

I also know that it is because of them that I have the attitude I have now. If it were not for Natalee and Karlee laying the foundation for me, I would probably think of Little much differently and probably be absorbed in grief and tears. I have my girls to thank for that.

I was married to their dad for thirteen years, and then we divorced. It was hard on all of us. I wish things could have gone differently. I wish none of what happened had to happen, but again it was one of the things in my life that has played a part in making me stronger.

There's one more thing that has made me look back and say, "Oh, now I understand." We all have those times in our lives; I'm not any different. When we're in them, we think it's the worst possible thing that can happen to us. It's until we're older and wiser that the "a-ha" moment comes and we realize it was all the way it was supposed to be.

Natalee, Karlee, and I were on our own for several years until Big Robert came into our lives. One blind date and a bowl of pasta later, poor Big Rob was becoming part of our tribe. I say "poor" because he had no idea what he was signing up for. He was a kind and gentle man who brought a lot of light and laughs to our home. He was thirty-five years old at the time we met and didn't have children of his own. I think he found the girls to be a lot of fun and very entertaining. We all got along really well, and Rob and I were on our way to becoming one.

Then, on April 11, 1996, we welcomed Little. Born at ten pounds and three ounces, he became the focal point of the house. At first, Natalee didn't take well to the newcomer stealing her spotlight as the first-born, but she got over it in time. Now we had two on their way to college and a newborn in the house. The girls were fantastic and helped us out a lot. We were all loving and enjoying the new baby very much. The girls got a good lesson in second-hand mothering and saw what it takes to raise a child. They also grew close to Little and fell madly in love with him.

Little developed normally for the first twelve months of his life. Then he started to do things I'd never seen before in a child. At the same time, he started losing all of the normal things he had developed. His speech was one of the first things to go. He went from saying "Mama," "Dada," and "bye-bye" to making noises that sounded like wild monkeys and dolphins.

Unlike many children with autism, he never regained his speech. He started to detach from all of us. He started to walk at thirteen months but fell often, much more often than other babies his age. I later learned that this was called an awkward gait, and that some children with neurological problems have difficulty walking.

He would jump on my bed for hours, but without looking happy about it. He would walk in patterns around the house. When I took him outside, he would head down the front sidewalk, touch the same plant, turn right, touch the metal drain on the ground, walk a few more steps and touch the cable to the light pole, continue on and touch the neighbor's sprinkler head, and so on. This was one, two, or even three times; this was every day for months and months. He wouldn't even notice the sound of a plane flying overhead or pay attention to a fire truck roaring down the street. It was as though he were on his mission and totally focused on getting his task done.

He also had a fixation on videos. He would watch them over and over, though he didn't watch regular TV shows. He was not interested in Barney on the actual TV show, but he would watch him on his VHS tapes. He would rewind every ten seconds or so and watch the same parts over and over. This too, I learned later on, was a sign of autism.

The neurologist told me that to children with autism videos are the drug of choice. When I asked him why, he said it's because they have control and there are no surprises; they know what's coming up next and this is very comforting to a child who is unsure of the world around him. He would flap his hands and get up on his tiptoes whenever he was excited about something and yell out really loudly at the same time. He was very picky about what he ate and would eat only foods with certain textures. He showed no interest in playing with other children, and to this day he has never played with another child. His sleep patterns became unpredictable; Rob and I were left to take turns with him during the night. It was exhausting and relentless.

We couldn't even take in what was happening because it was all happening so fast. I was not alarmed, though, because I didn't know any better. I didn't know I was looking at autism. I just knew that what Little was doing was different from what I was seeing other kids his age do. I didn't know how I was going to explain it all to his pediatrician, so I thought if I took pictures and videotaped it all I could describe better to him. Of course, I didn't know I would later use all of those pictures and videotapes to help college students better understand what autism looks like in a very young child.

Around the same time, two of my sisters-in-law started talking to each other about Little. They were concerned. Both of them had children. Both suspected autism but didn't have the heart to tell me.

Follow the Yellow Brick Road

At Little Robert's sixteen-month check up, I told our pediatrician (a less famous "Dr. Phil"), "Phil, he's doing all these different things and he's not talking anymore." As I continued on, I could see his face changing; finally he said, "OK, here's what I would like you to do. Go home and really work with little Robert. Try to get him to say at least six words, and see if you can get him to identify a body part." He then told me he wanted to see Little again at twenty-one months.

So I went home and started to work with him like a madwoman. I wasn't having a lot of luck and was beginning to think I had lost my touch as a mother. I thought that maybe by age thirty-eight I just didn't have the gift anymore. I enrolled him in Gymboree to get him around other children and their moms, thinking they could help me.

The first class pretty much told me it wasn't going to be as easy as I thought. The director of the program brought out "Jimbo," the Gymboree clown. The kids were all in free-play time so they were running around having a blast. Little fit right in with that activity, so everything was fine. Then the director yelled, "OK, play time is over; can you all come sit in the circle and help Jimbo? Jimbo has lost his mommy and he needs help finding her."

All the other kids in the class stopped what they were doing and headed toward her with very concerned looks on their face. One by one, they came into the circle. Little, on the other hand, was paying absolutely no attention to her request. He was not the least concerned about 'ole Jimbo. Little wouldn't sit in the circle. He didn't respond to anything the director said, or join the other children in any way. It was an eye-opening experience.

Little's twenty-one-month check-up came, and I felt no desire to keep the appointment. I felt like a failure not only because I hadn't succeeded in getting him to say six words but because everything had gotten much worse. Little was totally detached now, in a world of his own. It was as if someone had come into our house and swapped babies with us.

When we went to see Dr. Phil, I explained everything to him. He could see what was happening with Little, so he took us into his private office and told us he wanted us to see a neurologist.

About a month later, we were at Miami Children's Hospital. During our thirty-minute appointment, the neurologist asked what seemed like a million rapid-fire questions. He examined Little from head to toe. His assessment: "Mr. and Mrs. Becerra, this is what I'm writing on your son's chart. I'm writing that he is severely speech-delayed. I'm writing that he is severely developmentally delayed, and I'm writing that he is severely socially delayed." Then he looked up. I said, "What does that mean?" He said, "It means your son is clearly in the spectrum of autism."

At that moment, I went to the only resource I had on autism in my brain: the movie *Rainman*. Flashbacks from scenes in the movie started racing through my mind as I was still taking this all in. I knew the film had a powerful impact on me.

Thinking about it again brought me instant comfort and helped me think positively right away, even as the doctor was still standing in the room seeming to be dreading the news he was delivering. In my heart at that moment, I didn't think of Little as a tragedy. I thought of him as a precious and unique soul. Instinctively, I knew that this was going to change the course of the traditional role I had in my head about being a mother. I knew my destiny with him was going to follow a path I had never taken, and somewhere inside I knew it was all going to be OK.

Diagnostic papers in hand, we started down what seemed like the yellow brick road, except that instead of just one wizard we found many wise men and women. One of our early encounters was with Barry and Samahria Kaufman. They helped us understand Robert's mind, and more important how to respect him while teaching him at the same time. This was followed by Barry Prizant, whose wise words were, "Develop the emotional side of these children first and focus on the academics after, because it's almost impossible to achieve those in reverse." Because of that advice, we have the very loving and secure little boy that little Robert is today. Then came a public television documentary we watched, called "Come Back Jack," which showed the Parish family struggling to find something that could work for their child (see Chapter Thirteen). That led us to Arnold Miller and his wife, Eileen Miller (see Chapter Two). The Miller Method of working with children by elevating them off the ground is pure genius, and the Millers have our highest respect.

Steven Shore is a man with autism who holds an Ed.D., or Doctor of Education degree (see Chapter Six). I asked him once what he attributes his success to and he gave me his answer in less than one second: "My parents; their acceptance and belief in me got me to where I am today." As a mother, when I heard that, I melted.

Author Annabel Stehli's tireless efforts have showed us that the path might be bumpy, but to keep going. Michael Alessandri's brilliance and dedication to families helps all of us feel less alone. Of course, I have to add the families we've met who have children with autism. It's difficult to describe the impact they've had on us, but I will tell you that the deep-rooted kinship we share is something that never even needs to be spoken. Those are just some of the wizards we've come across on this road who have guided us with their wisdom. But just as in the movie *The Wizard of Oz,* where Dorothy finds out that what she was looking for she had all the time, I think what we set out in search of we actually had all the time too. It was right there in front of us in the form of a little boy who really just wants to be loved. It wasn't a *cure* he was hoping for us to find; it was love, and we had it the whole time.

In the children's section of a bookstore once, a little old man was reading a story to a large group of kids. When he saw us walk in, he motioned for me to bring Little over to join the group. I said in a loud whisper, "I would love to but it's hard for him to sit that long." He waved that it was OK and kept reading. When he finished, he came up to me and said, "I noticed your son. What is it that he has?" I told him. He asked me what autism was, and I briefly explained it. He then asked me how one goes about helping a child with autism. I told him there were a lot of things now a parent can do. In fact, I said, there are so many things it's hard to pick. I told him I have a sort of path of my own in mind, and that I'm going with my gut and hoping I have picked the right one. He told me he wrote poetry and asked me for my address. He said he was going to send me a poem he had written that he thought would be perfect for me.

A few days later, his poem arrived in the mail. The cover page said, "Dear Teresa: it was nice meeting you and seeing the love vibrating between you and your son. May it generate happiness for you forever."

> From my valley of indecision
> I saw the mountaintop. . . .
> Yearned to reach its pinnacle . . .
> but turned in confusion
> at the profusion
> of roads
> Which, I wondered,
> is the right one?
> Had I looked with my heart
> instead of my eyes,
> I would have known
> they all were.
>
> **—Ben Wakes**

I think Ben hit it right on the head. It doesn't matter which road you take as a parent. Each one is the right one.

Those mini-encounters started becoming part of my life with Little. Being with him has opened me up to other people. I feel differently about people now. I have a lot more understanding and compassion; I'm not afraid of people anymore. I feel good when I share my feelings with them, and I attribute that to watching Little open people's hearts every day. He's allowed me to see that we're all so human.

Here and Now

As the years passed, I developed a deep respect for Little's autism. I hold it sacred in my heart and I love his autism as much as I love him. He is the purest form of human being I know. He doesn't see color or religion in people; he sees only a person. He doesn't care if you are the president of the United States or a man who collects spare change on the street. It's not in him to be mean or hurt a person on purpose.

One of the most beautiful qualities I admire in Little is that he doesn't feel the need to live by society's rules. He is true to himself. He lives in the moment and doesn't worry about the day. He doesn't have a weekly agenda or yearly plan, and he has taught me not to have one either. The moments are why we're here. If the tomorrows come, they're just a plus.

Little has made me step back, step out of myself, and look at the bigger picture. He's showed me how to find inner peace—no small gift. He's inspired me to do things I never would have had the courage to do.

I live my passion now. I speak to hundreds of people every year about autism. I want to help everyone understand autism on a different level from what they might read in a book.

I have a little boy who doesn't speak, yet he moves every person around him. He teaches without the words I have to use. I try my hardest to translate how he makes me feel, but I often find it indescribable. It's overwhelming at times and brings me to tears.

I really want to help everyone who comes into contact with these special children understand that the best way to reach them is through respect. It's a lot like the techniques the "horse whisperer" uses. You can break these precious souls down to get them to conform, or you can gently whisper and get the same results but also maintain their free spirit and who they are intact. Working with children with autism or raising a child with autism is an art form; if done right, you'll have the honor of looking into the window of a mind that not many will ever get the chance to see.

At night, when I lie down next to Little and watch him fall asleep, it's an incredible feeling. I've done my job for the day. I've kept him safe and alive one more day. Tomorrow will be here soon enough, and I know I need to get my sleep.

I crack a little smile as I say to myself, "It's just a little autism; it's just a little autism."

10

ACCEPTANCE
IN WAVES

[BY ROBERT BECERRA]

(Father of "Little Robert," Robert Becerra has, like many dads of ASD children, often struggled with the emotional repercussions of the diagnosis. This piece is a companion to the preceding chapter, written by Robert's wife, Teresa. —RP)

I was childless when I met my wife. She had two teenage girls, and they became my stepdaughters and a source of wonder, amusement, and eventually pride for me.

I am grateful that we met and that we were all able to form a family together. Things moved very quickly, and before long a new life was on its way into ours. To say that I was unprepared for parenthood is the understatement of the year. I stared at the ultrasound in disbelief and awe.

I fell in love with Little Robert on his second night home from the hospital. He was restless and having a hard time sleeping, and I walked him around the house, holding him to my shoulder. Finally, he settled down and we fell asleep together on the couch. I had my feet up on the coffee table, and he lay on my chest. Watching him breathe, I felt the most overpowering sensation of love and protectiveness I had ever known.

He was a big baby and grew quickly. Early on, he hit all his developmental milestones and all was well. But, then the strange behaviors began—the flapping and shouting, the bouncing on his tiptoes. The repetitive moving around the house and touching the same objects in sequence. The hours of staring at videos and wanting nothing else.

When he lost the modest amount of speech he had gained, we really began to worry; eventually we found ourselves in a neurological consultation. The moment Little Robert was diagnosed with autism, I had no reaction whatsoever. I went numb inside. That night, I woke up crying at three in the morning. I was actually crying in my sleep. I walked outside and smoked cigarette after cigarette and cried until I had cried myself out.

Unlike my wife, who had romantic images of *Rainman* in her head, I knew that the chances of his being high functioning were slight. All that kept going through my head were the things he would never be and never do. The little word *autism* had turned my life upside down, and it turned my strange and adorable little boy into a diagnosis—a pathology. It took months before I could see him as a person again.

I spent days on the Internet looking for a solution. Surely there was a biological or surgical intervention that could fix this thing. My search turned up nothing. Then, in a bookstore, a title caught my eye: *Son Rise: The Miracle Continues*. I devoured the book. Here was a case of a person who had recovered from autism. Here was the solution. We could finally fix him. I missed the point of the book entirely. Or, maybe not entirely. At least I felt I had received permission to stop looking at him as something that needed to be fixed and instead see him as a person, although a very different one.

We traveled to Massachusetts and spent the week learning how to create a home-based therapy program grounded on acceptance and cooperation.

I became fixated on doing it right and forgot all about the prevailing admonition that if one is not happy, one has little chance of helping a child with autism.

We started the program, and I found quickly that I could not practice what *Son Rise* preached. Unable to maintain a high degree of acceptance, I could not even remain present enough to work with my son in the room. Thanks to my wife and the relationship she cultivated with local schools, volunteers came and went. We learned about the Miller Method and incorporated it into our home-based program. As time passed, more information became available about the physiological causes of autism, and we tried every cutting-edge biological intervention that was being promoted. We spent countless hours and tens of thousands of dollars. All of these things helped Little Robert to varying degrees, but nothing seemed to cure him.

In those days, I dealt with a lot of "if onlys." If only we could get the mercury out of his brain. If only we could heal his leaky gut. If only we could open his detoxification pathways. If only we could eliminate intestinal funguses. If only we could get him to point to what he wants with his index finger and thereby establish "theory of mind." One by one, the if-onlys grew.

Eventually, I gave up. I am no longer interested in the latest biological intervention. I feel we have done everything and tried everything. I definitely never want to try something that could harm him. All that is left now is acceptance, and helping him achieve his potential. I work on that daily.

Life with Little Robert, now ten years old, can be strange and all-consuming. The antics that my wife finds amusing sometimes cause me distress. I am a high-strung person by nature and am easily overstimulated. Life with autism is a constant bombardment of weirdness and disarray. Cell phones appear in washing machines in the middle of a cycle. TV remotes find their way into toilets. Appliances are unplugged and swung from their cords like pendulums. Entire closets full of clothes are removed from their hangers and thrown into full bathtubs of water. Shoes are thrown over balcony railings, shoelaces removed and the ends eaten off. Wallpaper gets peeled and bathtub caulking removed; paint chips are removed and eaten. All manner of things are picked up from the street and shoved into Little Robert's mouth: gum, leaves, mulch, paper. Chandeliers are swung on and full vases of water poured out onto sofas. Lights are turned off . . . and on . . .

and off . . . and on. Sliding door locks are carefully removed and flung into the lake for Daddy to retrieve on one of those rare days in Miami when the temperature is in the forties.

Don't get me wrong, I love my son. He is the most important thing in my life. Living with ASD can be a weird and disconcerting experience for a person like me who is easily overstimulated.

Luckily, I have my wife; her adoring acceptance is contagious enough that I can see what she sees just often enough to help me keep my sanity. I know Little Robert did not ask for this, and I know that he is always doing his best. I also know that as he gets older, he understands more and does better.

There are the rewards, too. Like going to the grocery store and having him push the cart and watching with amazement how he picks out the things that he likes from the shelves and carefully puts them into the shopping cart. I realize that he is just like every one of us, doing his best to take care of his needs.

His command of electronics is impressive. He can be handed any kind of VCR, DVD, or CD player and instantly figure out how it works. He looks carefully at the writing on a CD or tape and seems to know what it says so that he can identify which one he wants to listen to. It's a form of reading, and I hope that it will eventually lead to more.

He is very intelligent at figuring out how to get what he wants; faced with a lock or other obstacle, he will quickly find a way to defeat it and achieve his objective.

He is also warm, sensitive, and gentle. It is obvious that he loves us, even if he cannot say the words. Sometimes he comes up to me and looks into my eyes and throws his arms out to me, and my heart just melts. He also gives the best kisses in the world.

I do not relate well to people in general, which is much more of a challenge with someone who cannot speak and is limited in his interactions. I am also limited in my interactions. The one thing I can do is love Little Robert and be physically affectionate; that is my strength. He is not the slightest bit tactile-defensive, in part because he has been kissed and hugged and snuggled so many thousands of times in his short life.

I would not be telling the whole story though, if I did not mention my wife, Teresa. More than any therapy, more than any book I have read, she has taught me the true meaning of acceptance and love, and that they are absolute. She does not judge him; she celebrates Little Robert's differences in every possible way. She also works hard in spreading the word about acceptance and autism, to touch the lives and hearts of the next generation that will work with our children.

There is no way I could do this without her. She is our daily inspiration and light, and I appreciate her. I thank her for her unflagging patience and optimism.

I will not lie: sometimes, when I see all of the things that other dads do with typical ten-year-olds, Robert's autism breaks my heart. I become conscious of the limitations of our interactions and relationship. The only thing I know for sure is that we love each other and that we will get through what life sends us together. I continue to hope and pray that as he grows older he will become more available to me, and I to him.

My heart goes out to all parents and educators of children with autism. They deal with an enigma every day, and their dedication and love are not often directly reciprocated. They must trust that somewhere within the heart of the child there is a place that appreciates and loves, and that their efforts are appreciated, even if gratitude goes unspoken. That is acceptance at work and love in action. As long as acceptance and love are present, there is no need for tomorrow's cure, because the miracle is already here.

My favorite part of the day is getting Little Robert ready for bed. We lie down next to him and snuggle and tell him how much we love him. I know in those moments, beyond a shadow of a doubt, that he knows how much I care.

Acceptance for me comes in waves—those magical moments when all that I am aware of is how magical and fascinating he is, and how lucky I am to be his dad. When that happens, nothing else matters.

11

EVERYONE HAS A CHANCE TO GROW

[BY JACKIE MARQUETTE]

(With more than twenty years as a special educator and school consultant, Jackie found her professional inspiration close to home. Her son Trent is an adult with an ASD diagnosis. She recently received her Ph.D. from the University of Louisville. —RP)

How can we best guide teens and young adults diagnosed with autism spectrum disorders to live their lives as capably and fully as possible during adolescence and adult years?

As a parent of an adult with autism, and having taught high school students with various disabilities, I learned that those diagnosed with autism see in themselves what we see in them. Although academics may play a part in what a person eventually knows, it is indeed his or her strengths and the supports provided to meet needs that become most important.

Their most basic need mirrors all of ours: knowing they are valued for who they are.

I have always known that my mission as Trent's mother is to search for and connect him to settings, friendships, and interests that bring a meaningful experience. Throughout the years, the integrative outcomes have been mixed with success and setbacks. Yet when accomplishments were made—such as performing in front of a large audience with a high school chorus—I saw eagerness revealed in his sparkling eyes, which confirmed his self-worth, self-value.

I recall allowing Trent to go out with a peer, or with his job or community coach, and feeling fearful, wondering if he would be cooperative and get through the event without a problem. One of the best suggestions I can offer teachers and parents is to practice letting go in small ways. After a period of time, this will become more familiar and easier on both the child and parent. I discovered that as I stretched to emotionally let go of Trent so that he could experience or enjoy an outing without me, he eventually showed greater independence and self-reliance.

All youth must develop a positive sense of what their lives as adults will be like. Parents want good quality of life for their child with autism, and the first step is to form a vision of what they may become. Yet forming the vision in our mind becomes difficult when we rarely see positive examples of people with ASD living fully and independently. There are many definitions of quality of life. In my view, a person's quality of life boils down to being respected and finding acceptance in his or her own world.

Although stated simply, this definition offers tangible ideas on how this looks, and it differs with each individual according to his or her needs and preferences. Similar to "typical" teens, those in the autism spectrum need opportunities in the community to identify strengths, interests, and gifts. Most importantly, they need opportunities to practice these skills so that, when they reach adulthood, they will be better equipped to manage and enjoy their own lives. ASD children and adults need knowledge about negotiating life with the necessary supports in a world that tends not to appreciate their differences.

I once read that what is good for people without disabilities will generally be good for those with them, and something that is ordinarily bad for people without disabilities will be bad for people who have them.

It is possible to guide a teen or young adult to reach full community living with increased independence. During the past several years researching for my dissertation, I interviewed fifteen families who actively guided their son or daughter to reach independent living.

Their personal journeys can show the pathway that can inspire others. I see independent living defined as individuals who have a disability living at their highest capability level with the "supports" that help them participate in everyday living activities, such as having a job or living in an apartment or a house. A person who reaches "independent living" may do so with "few supports." Yet a person can also live "independently" with many "supports." Most importantly, "living independently" means *never* going it alone.

Although there were differences in the severity of the individuals' autism, in the state where they lived, and in their particular interests and gifts, I learned that the parents and educators who worked with these individuals were helped by setting goals early and initiating actions to secure supports that met personal needs.

In my own case, I recognized how Trent's experiences were similar to the young adults in the study, including the challenges faced, the joys gained from accomplishment, and the parental appreciation felt for the lessons learned despite the struggles. The bottom line for all of us: our child's happiness and self-value became the highest priority.

Trent

At this writing, my son Trent is thirty years old. He is employed at Meijer's, a large discount retail store, and has lived independently with a roommate for seven years. Trent is also a Kentucky juried artist and has a business exhibiting and selling his paintings at art fairs and in galleries. The life he has today did not just happen. In fact, if you knew Trent ten years ago, you would be surprised to see how far he has come. For sure, there were actions I pursued that led Trent forward on his journey. Most importantly, I tossed his "disability" label aside and, through a process of exploration, identified his strengths and gifts. I knew how critical it was that Trent have the necessary supports to help him participate and learn from his experiences among other peers. I embarked on a path to create and negotiate those supports. When Trent was three years old, he received a diagnosis of autism and was considered "severely or moderately disabled." Although he had significant language delay and exhibited many withdrawn behaviors, he was included in almost all of our family activities. Some extended family members were not understanding and merely tolerated his presence. At times, that really hurt.

Growing up with his two typical brothers gave Trent acceptance and some social contact with their friends, who were often around our house. Yet Trent did not have friends of his own. He was placed in self-contained special education classes but did participate in regular music and art classes.

The emphasis during Trent's high school years became employment because I advocated strongly for it. There is a link among having a job, living a higher quality of life, and independence. Trent had the privilege of job coach support, which allowed him to hold several paid jobs and prepared him for employment during his adult years.

After high school ended, both our lives spiraled downward quickly. It was not a smooth transition. For Trent, many changes occurred that caused him to plummet emotionally and socially, moving from:

- Being a student to being an adult

- The structure of the school day to many extra hours that had to be filled with a plan created by me

- Having a place to go each day to being confined to the house, unless I took him out or hired a community coach

- Seeing his brothers every day to watching them leave home for college or work

- Living with both parents to living with mom because of parental divorce

- Moving from our family home to another neighborhood

I was shocked to be in the middle of my son's transition crisis. I remember wondering why no one had told me how much impact this changing phase could have. I had prepared Trent and myself well for his transition during high school, but life had other plans after school ended.

The grocery store job Trent had during high school ended when we moved. This change frightened and confused him. I could see through his behavior that he was unsure about the security of his life and what was to become of him. I felt powerless to offer him the support he needed to have consistent daily structure.

I soon realized that I was not supposed to be the one who offered him daily structure. My job included accessing resources and creating supports to help Trent find his own identity, which had to be connected to something other than me; he needed purpose in each day.

Since Trent was a small child, I had a dream that he would live independently as an adult and have a job he loved. Now that he was a young man, all I could do was watch him react with fear and obsessive behaviors that virtually isolated both of us in our home. I knew that the way he was living did not reflect who he was inside. I knew he had value, and that through his behavior he was calling out for help. At this phase of my life, I had no other alternative but to leave my job and collect unemployment until I could figure out the next step.

I refused to lose hope. I knew if he were to get out of this crisis it would be up to me. That is, I would have to find the help and assistance and bring all the pieces together.

How did I begin? I became empowered through first retreating and taking care of myself. I put my needs first in order to establish rest and become grounded. Second, I revisited all the research I had read on best practices and principles in creating independent living. Third, I read how other people overcame their challenges in other areas, which further empowered me. I chose to act on Trent's behalf and be his voice, but in a new, improved, age-appropriate way.

I accepted help from my brother and my friends; I held monthly person-centered-planning meetings, inviting all who could assist in creating Trent's new adult life. I assertively sought support, and a supported living grant to request funding to secure these supports. With all this networking, luckily a young man named Jason was referred to Trent as a community coach.

He worked out so well for Trent that he later accepted the job as his live-in roommate and supporter.

I recall having mixed feelings, being elated and frightened when I left our home and Jason moved in with Trent. For the first time in my life, I could go to the drug store and not arrange for someone to stay with Trent or rush to get home because he was alone. This freedom was wonderful. But I struggled with living alone in an apartment and preparing my own evening meal without Trent.

Trent resisted his new independent life. I recall driving my car into his driveway every day after work and noticing him standing at his front door waiting for me.

With time and planned daily tasks, Trent began to adapt and settle into his home and the community. I sought ways to reassure him that his family had not left him. In conversation during our long weekend visits, I always painted an idyllic picture of how his life would be as a man with a job, spending money, paying his bills, enjoying going out to restaurants and movies, meeting new people, and even going on vacation.

One year after adapting to independent life, Trent began exploring art as an activity. Because art classes catered to children or artists who were supposedly advanced, I hired a university art student to come to Trent's house. The purpose of their art activities was to find a hobby that would enhance his quality of life.

It was during these at-home sessions we discovered Trent's gift of creating beautiful abstract expressionistic paintings. Today, he is a well-known artist and enjoys all that it brings him: art shows, juried street fairs, and new artist friends.

With supports, Trent has discovered his value and contribution to the world. His functioning level has increased, thanks to those supports, because he has had the experience of learning what he can do and seeing the person he could become.

The Importance of Supports

Before I began to seek supports for Trent, I first had to believe that living fully in the community was valuable and achievable. In other words, I let go of his "disability" label. The more severe a disability label is, the more likely it is to become a major factor in keeping an individual with ASD from entering the community.

It is common practice for people with moderate to severe disability to work in a sheltered workshop or day program excluding that person from the community. I refused to allow all the negatives that autism represents to be a driving force that would lead Trent to a sheltered environment. All the principles in community living and beliefs about the strengths and capability in people with disability were the foundation for the goals and supports I negotiated.

In my view, a person's functioning level, high or low, should not be a criterion for determining whether to strive for community participation, independent living, or choosing a life that is uniquely his own. Labels are for service and program funding. As a wise person once said, "Labels are for cans, not people."

Everyone's Gift Counts

All youth with ASD need parents and professionals to be their "believing mirrors," reflecting their gifts, capabilities, and strengths. It is vitally important we see them as whole people, with gifts to share and disability limitations to accept.

Every person with ASD can contribute something of value to our world. For all of us, developing a strength or gift and using it—whether in employment or leisure—affirms one's self-value and acceptance within the community. In my research, I discovered that higher capability and personal growth also occur when people enjoy using the best they have to give.

Martin Seligman, an internationally known psychologist and researcher, suggests that a person's gift or talent is innate, though it requires personal choice to develop it. The gift could be singing in perfect pitch, running at lightning speed, or painting a beautiful picture. Strong visual thinking skills and the ability to categorize are also gifts, ones that are often strong attributes of children with ASD.

Seligman says that strengths are attributes that anyone can develop, such as helping or comforting others and showing loyalty; they can be built upon with time and effort. Although most individuals with ASD need supports to participate, experience and involvement can reveal the person's gift or strength, and this in turn draws people together in a group that is based on the interest.

Pat Danielson, an adult with a physical disability, once said that we need to guide youths to cultivate an attitude of "I belong here. I am an important part of life."

Walking with Others

Trent's diagnosis and journey into adulthood inspired me to explore how other families guided their children with ASD into community living and adulthood. I learned a lot of important lessons about transitions into adulthood from my research, which became my Ph.D. dissertation at the University of Louisville. Three of these families touched my heart.

MELISSA

Melissa has an autism spectrum diagnosis. Today, she attends a Baptist college and works in a day care facility because she loves playing with and caring for babies and small children. She is majoring in sociology. Her goal is to become an officer with the Federal Emergency Management Agency (FEMA).

Many years ago, no one—not even her parents—believed she would ever accomplish what she has. When Melissa was born, doctors predicted she would not live past the age of ten. She was labeled "severely mentally retarded and autistic." Melissa had many health problems, including extreme allergies and blood clotting disorders. But her parents had expectations that she would be as responsible and capable as possible, no matter what it looked like. They encouraged her to be self-sufficient and prompted her to solve simple problems.

Her educational experience included placement in self-contained classrooms. In high school, she participated in a job try-out program and earned a certificate for completion. Shortly after graduation, Melissa tried to get a job, but no one would hire her because she did not have a high school diploma. She asked her mother to go with her to sign up for an adult education class to earn a GED. She eventually achieved a passing score. The next year, she convinced her mother to help her prepare for the ACT test. After several tries, she obtained a score that, though low, was enough to enable her to enter college. Melissa and her mother then toured several colleges throughout the state and chose the school she now attends. A funny thing happened, her mother laughed: "The college she applied for offered her a one-year scholarship because her grades were all A's. No one there noticed she was in special education."

Melissa has been taking one or two classes each semester while working part-time. Her goal for a career changed after hurricanes Ivan and Katrina hit the gulf coast. Melissa was the first to volunteer each time her church called for a group to help. She found love in helping people within the support of her church. She would do any task, from picking up trash to moving heavy items. She most enjoyed distributing basic daily items to people in need. Her mother is continually surprised at Melissa's personal growth and has no doubt that she will eventually have a career with FEMA.

JAMES

James lives independently in a small upstairs apartment in his mother's house. According to his mother, he has autism, is very low-functioning, and has an IQ measuring in the low twenties. But his disability did not change his mother's dream that he would live fully in the community. His mother has been a strong advocate and was adamant that he have a high quality of life and access to opportunities where he could offer a contribution regardless of his disability. He is served by an agency to help him live independently and has assistants and friends who introduce him to a variety of activities in the community. They also support him in his part-time job at a preschool.

James's mother believes her son's autism diagnosis has no relevance to what he pursues during his life. His supporters identified his strength, which is staying with all the steps of a task (once he has learned it) through final completion and strong enjoyment of young children and babies. He loves the sound of their laughter and cries.

So how do those skills and strengths translate into a job? James prepares two long tables for snack time at a preschool, placing tablecloths, setting out paper products, putting cookies and fruit in trays, and pouring the juice. The excitement begins when the children run in for their snack, because they are so eager to see him. His mother says, "They laugh, call him Uncle James, and give him big hugs." His presence and the work he does are definitely of value to the children.

Unfortunately, James's life was not always this fulfilled. His mother says he was denied even the most basic services during the school years. School personnel wanted to hide him from other students in the regular classroom setting and refused to let him participate in school events. Her experience was an uphill battle throughout all the school years.

Today, James is thirty and using his best strengths to make preschool children happy and grateful for his services during snack time. Most importantly, he is doing what he loves and enjoys, and is making connections and friendships. The support from people who assist him allows him to make a community contribution and enjoy his at-work experiences. He is living a life valued for its uniqueness and contribution.

BILL

Bill is twenty-eight years old, has high functioning autism, and lives in his own apartment. Bill's mother died when he was just five. He was diagnosed with ADHD and a learning disability during his early elementary school years. Because Bill had an extreme speech disorder, his dad hired private speech therapists to work with his son. His grandmother drew close to him after his mother died, but because of one negative comment she made about the way he talked, Bill disliked her for the next fifteen years.

Despite his high level of intelligence, the K–12 school years were difficult for Bill. His behavior was disruptive; he had no friends. When he arrived in middle school, his dad arranged for him to be tested by a psychiatrist. Bill was labeled with an "attachment disorder," primarily because of his mother's premature death. Eventually, this proved to be an inaccurate diagnosis. At the age of seventeen, after another evaluation, he was diagnosed with autism.

In high school, his withdrawn and sometimes aggressive behavior escalated. He pleaded with a fellow student to help him burn down their high school; fortunately, it did not happen. He also tried to commit suicide. Several times, Bill was summoned to juvenile court.

Despite all his challenges, Bill had a lot of positive things going for him. He excelled in math and loved social studies, primarily because a teacher took the time to connect with Bill's interest in helping the disadvantaged people of the world.

After graduating from high school, he gave college a try. His goal was to get a degree in business. He achieved 60 college credit hours with a 2.2 GPA. The on-campus life, however, became too much for Bill to manage. Not long after he gave up on school, his grandmother died. He realized then what an extraordinary impact she had had on his life. Despite Bill's issues with her critiquing his ability to pronounce words, he appreciated her encouragement to pursue a career where he could apply his mathematical knowledge. She often suggested that Bill apply for employment at the Internal Revenue Service.

Within a month after his grandmother's death, he went to the IRS, applied for a job, and was hired. Today, he enjoys his independent life with peer connections through work and participating in spectator sporting events. He also travels to nearby cities independently, attending concerts of his favorite bands.

His dad says proudly, "Not too bad for a child whose mother died at five, who had a learning disability and autism, and who struggled educationally and socially."

See the Whole Person

When working with someone in the autism spectrum, it is important to gather up all the scattered pieces and see how they can come together for the individual. Find the connecting thread that can link the strength, skill, or gift to areas for employment, leisure, or basic community living.

See the whole person—the positive attributes and the limitations.

Tony Attwood, an expert and researcher in the field of autism, said, "People with autism can create with full emotion in music or art that which they cannot show in relationships."

Educators and parents sometimes pursue habits of teaching or care giving that may limit a child or adult's potential (for example, doing too much for the person). Seek new ways of support that can promote the individual's capability and self-reliance. Meet needs by providing supports so he or she can explore and participate in specific areas of interest.

Teens and young adults with ASD need professionals and families to collaborate and create programs where mentors or community coaches can find many different kinds of supports to help them participate in society and achieve increased personal growth.

Everyone should have a chance to grow and create ways the individual can realize self-respect and self-acceptance.

12

GRASS IN THE WIND

[BY KRISTINA CHEW]

(Kristina Chew's son, Charlie, has been a focal point of her writing for many years. Along with being Charlie's mom, Kristina is a passionate advocate for children carrying an ASD diagnosis. She holds a Ph.D. and is a classics professor at St. Peter's College in northern New Jersey. —RP)

"Bread!" Charlie giggled to his speech therapist as he rounded his lips in his oral-motor exercises. "Da shooszon," he said. (Translation: "Let's wrap things up; I'm going to put my shoes on.")

After speech therapy, we filled up the "black car" with "gazzz" and stopped at "liberry," where I found a DVD on the Romans to show my class after we had discussed the rise of Caesar. Then we headed to the grocery store, where Charlie, as he has for the past year, went to look at the cupcakes and cookies in the bakery section—only to look, as he knows he is to do.

So, when I turned around to find Charlie with a whipped-cream finger going from inside the plastic cake container to his mouth, I said to myself, "OK, he has been talking about cake a lot lately. I should have been watching."

Charlie already had the nervous pull to his face when I asked him for the cake container, which was ever so slowly handed over. "You know you need to wait till we're home to eat food from the store," I said.

The sushi case is right next to the bakery section of this grocery store, so I added that I did not think he could get sushi today as a result. Charlie looked at me and served up what I like to call a little cry.

Suddenly and without warning, the little cry exploded into a much louder cry.

He hit the floor, flipped over on his back, and began banging his head hard against the floor. I quickly dove down with him, placing one hand and then both beneath the back of his head. At school, he is directed to lie on a mat at such times; he usually calms in a minute. In the grocery store, the floor was the only option, and I simply stayed there with Charlie. I waited for the little-cry-turned-louder-cry to pass.

For two-plus years, from age seven to nine, this kind of thing happened a few times every day.

My motherly instincts told me that he would get through it faster if I could let the rage or strickenness or whatever pass out of his body in waves of energy I would try to lean along with. This is why only my hands were between the cold, waxed floor and his banging head.

Not long after Charlie's meltdown began, a woman who introduced herself as a physician's assistant asked very discreetly if any medical assistance was needed. I said (so evenly that in retrospect I am surprised), "My son has autism."

A few minutes passed, and a concerned grandmotherly woman came over and muttered what sounded like "the police are coming." I looked at her as calmly as I could and repeated my declaration, "My son has autism," adding, "There's really no need for the police. He's calming down."

Proving my point, Charlie slowly lifted himself up, clutching our shopping basket for dear life. He continued to cry beyond woebegone as we walked through the store, exploring the aisles for our usual assortment of good things to eat and drink. While more shoppers noticed our plight, I continued to assure him everything was going to be all right, hoping of course that our audience would get the message as well.

We arrived in the produce section, where he selected half a watermelon. Then, in front of the freezer, he agreed to fish for dinner. I was struck by the fact that he made no effort to stand in front of the open case piled high with bags of frozen french fries.

Even though our situation had calmed, Charlie and I were undoubtedly quite the discombobulated sight. He was still clutching the basket for dear life. I, with cake container in one hand, was walking awkwardly, thanks to a shoe strap broken in the commotion of the floor tantrum. We arrived at the checkout line, welcomed by more curious onlookers. Charlie tried to lift the basket onto the conveyor belt. I lent a hand.

"Just put it all up there," said the woman in line behind us to her teenage son, whose hair was long, rumpled, and stuffed under his sweatshirt hood, his posture slack.

He mumbled a few words and leaned down to pick up a large container of ruby red grapefruit juice, which did not make it to the counter. "What did I tell you!" said the mom, turning half-around; "My son spilled a container of juice in aisle three!"

"Why did you have to tell her that?" asked the son.

"Why do you have to be this way?" challenged the mother.

"Listen, I think you don't." The son stopped himself, probably realizing the at-home consequences of his smart mouth. Their shopping basket was full of several yellowish yogurt containers, another ruby red juice, and something else along the same color scheme. The son shrugged and very slowly placed the items on the conveyor belt as Charlie and I each took a bag and headed for the door.

I glanced back at the dysfunctional pair and for a brief moment felt a pang of jealousy. Her plight with her son seemed so innocuous compared to mine. If only Charlie challenged me with his words, instead of his behavior. That would be so easy.

As we drove home, I thought about how, instead of bracing my body against Charlie's twisting back and fighting with every last ounce of strength I do not have to keep him still and stop his head from hitting the floor, I had tried to shape myself along with the flow of his energy—leaning back in, or with, or together with, his body, which during these moments is practically sparking with desperation.

His most recent public outburst certainly took less out of me than attempts in previous years to hang on to my thrashing son. I am sure I used to hold on so hard because of my own, most despairing fear: "What will I do when he gets big? When he is bigger than me?"

"The grass must bend, when the wind blows across it."
—Confucius, Analects XII.19

Autism is about the art of learning to let go. Learning how to just be with Charlie.

Once when he was a two-year-old determined to walk in only one direction down the street, and a five-year-old buzzing and humming as he ran up and down the aisles of Target with me hurrying red-faced after him determined that he act "appropriately" in public, I used to say to myself, "He *will* do this the right way" and "He has to do this right, and now."

As the years passed, it is not only the distance between Charlie's head and my shoulder but also his own abilities, his mind, and his understanding that have grown, far beyond what I once thought possible. At one time I used to think, "Charlie must grow up according to certain developmental milestones, according to certain dictates." Now I see that he must grow up as he can, just as a dandelion makes do with whatever nourishment and space it gets from a crack in the sidewalk.

As a young person labeled with the difference of autism, Charlie has to grow up as he can in the too-small space society allots to him. Rather than making myself yet another imposing force telling him to bend this way or that, I'm learning how to bend with him. It's not always easy; the contorted positions are sometimes painful.

Charlie is as he is. He is Charlie. I am his mom, the one who must bend. When I do bend, what I learn cannot be contained in all the lost volumes of the ancient library of Alexandria. What I learn is something not written in any psychology textbook, or autism handbook, or treatment protocol. Thanks to many long hours of being together, I know that there is no better autism teacher than my son.

I have been slowly learning how to swim in the ocean waves, thanks to watching Charlie. Too often I have made the mistake of standing up to a wave, a greater power, and as proof of my folly I am smashed mercilessly on the sand and shells. When Charlie plays in the ocean, he swims right into the waves. When a wave comes behind him, he cocks his head a bit and adjusts his body so that he goes under the wave (under the water), or so that he fits right into the wave.

In other words, he makes himself go from being the grass into becoming the wind moving over it.

13

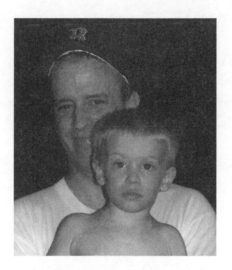

NOW FOR
OUR FEATURE
PRESENTATION

[BY ROBERT PARISH]

Jack jams a VHS tape into the food-stained TV/VCR combo.

    Jack presses Play.

    Jack presses Pause.

Jack presses Rewind.

Jack turns the volume up.

Jack closes one eye.

Jack presses Fast Forward.

Jack gets up.

Jack sits down.

Jack gets up.

Jack flaps his arms.

Jack verbalizes a series of sounds that mean something only to him.

Jack darts back to the TV/VCR combo.

Jack jumps.

Jack runs to a TV/VCR combo in another room.

Jack presses Fast Forward.

Jack presses Rewind.

Jack sits down.

Jack gets up.

Jack presses Eject.

Jack grabs another tape.

Jack jumps on my lap.

Jack jams the new tape into the TV/VCR combo.

Jack's dad (that's me) watches in amazement, amusement, and on bad days disappointment.

"And now for our feature presentation," bellows the deep-voiced Walt Disney announcer man.

And now for our feature presentation," I say, resonating from the depths of my diaphragm.

Jack turns and places his larger-than-I-can-believe right hand on my cheek.

Jack's big blue eyes plead for another over-the-top announcement from the old man.

"And now for our feature presentation," I roar.

Jack laughs.

"More," he says.

"No, Jack," I say. "Let's hear your voice!"

"And now for our feature presentation," he mumbles in his always surprisingly deep voice, laughing.

Jack gets up.

Jack runs off.

Tigger bounces and sings in the distance.

Before long, Jack's back.

"And now for?" he asks.

"Our feature presentation!" I respond.

And so it goes.

On and on.

On and on.

On and on.

Until my teenage son is ready to move to the next thing, which can happen at any moment.

Jackie, Can You Hear Me?

First and foremost, I'm a dad. I have four children, all of whom are of course amazing. Each has been blessed with an inspiring abundance of unique talents and gifts. The two oldest, Graham and Ryan, are "launched," pursuing careers that require enormous patience and empathy. My only daughter, Courtney, is in high school, wowing teachers, coaches, and way too many teenage boys with her intellect, athleticism, and beauty.

My youngest, the occasionally VCR-obsessed Jack Michael, is in many ways beyond amazing. For lack of a better term, let's call him very special.

Our father-and-son journey, which recently entered its fifteenth year, has been moving, uneasy, empowering, depressing, profound, disturbing, confusing, instructive, destructive, and life-changing.

Jack emerged into our world at exactly 9:30 P.M., Eastern Standard Time, on February 3, 1993. A baby of the night, his birth seemed especially peaceful, profound, and beautiful. He showed up smiling, hitting the pediatric "APGAR" (a simple, visual method of determining the health of a newborn) scale at a perfect 10.

Once his little feet were out, his bright blue eyes glistening under the intensity of the lights—and Jack was resting comfortably on his mother's stomach—I was strongly encouraged by an almost applauding delivery room staff to cut his umbilical cord. After much coaxing, I took the sterile surgical scissors in my surprisingly shaky right hand. Little did I realize that I was about to physically release my youngest son into a world that he would become mostly uninterested in before his second birthday.

All systems were go ("He's such a good baby!" "How cute!" "What a big smile!") during Jack's first sixteen months. He walked early and hit his developmental milestones right on time. His speed and agility were impressive. Trying not to sound like the typical proud dad, I must say Jack was incredibly handsome. His baby dark hair quickly turned blonde, which complemented his fair skin and piercing eyes.

Unlike his older brothers and sister, who all had various forms of early-year fussy-ness, Jack was mostly happy, easy to please, engaged, and often enthralled with his parents and three older siblings. Suddenly, it seemed, he began to fall apart cognitively and emotionally. He became mostly silent, disengaged, and unresponsive.

Jack also developed a number of bizarre, obsessive-compulsive interests, presented here in no particular order: wading in our twenty-gallon playroom fish tank, slamming his body as hard as he could into any chair or couch, banging his sippy cups on hard surfaces, and fast-forwarding and rewinding with action-packed videotapes.

After a couple of very difficult weeks of unexpected everything— including a middle-of-the-night meltdown, where Jack smeared the brown contents of his diaper all over the wall of his bedroom—his mother and I realized something was terribly wrong. "Do you think he's deaf?" was one of the first questions Diane and I asked our pediatrician. Hundreds of others followed, including "Do you think our son could have autism?" Most—especially that one—were greeted with smiles and condescending responses: "Be patient, boys always develop more slowly than girls." "Stop worrying so much. He'll grow out of it." "Why do you want something to be wrong with him?"

After Diane saw Dan Marino and his family on ABC's *Good Morning America* talking about autism, we finally had a solid perspective, and some ammunition to take to Jack's doctor. We pushed for a referral to a center in Cincinnati with a great reputation for diagnosing and treating every handicap under the sun.

Just a Label?

On February 27, 1996, four days before my forty-fifth birthday, three-year-old Jack Parish was labeled with what's now most often called an autism spectrum disorder (ASD). Back then, the often-misinformed medical community delivered the diagnosis of autism as if it were a death sentence.

The four-week evaluation process was a subjective, sporadic, disorganized, confidence-killing mess. The battery of tests, conducted by well-meaning professionals, made little sense to Diane and me, and absolutely none to our son. Of course, it was expensive, with insurance covering only a small portion of the cost.

When the news flash regarding Jack's "disability" was finally tossed out in a dimly lit conference room by a careless, downright bedside-manner-lacking developmental "specialist," I was torn. And I was very angry. Should I dart across the room, grab her voluminous file folder, check the name on the tab ("She can't be talking about my son!"), and then throw every badly written, poorly researched document out the window? Or should I hide under the table and cry? Of course, I did neither.

Nearly every moment of our two-hour meeting is a blank. Once I heard Jack's diagnosis, my eyes glazed over. Like most parents, face to face with autism for the first time, I was totally in denial. The one and only vivid memory I have is the doctor's judgment that Jack's "handicap" was especially severe, and that we should immediately begin looking for "another place for him to live."

Sadly, the nasty little lab-coated woman with M.D. after her name wasn't talking about new digs for our family. Her ill-chosen words got the Parish ASD adventure off to a terrifying start. My personal freak-out sent me diving, head first, into depths of despair I had never known. When I wasn't tearing up, I was sullen, distant, distracted, disagreeable, and (as my older typical sons would say) "a real dick."

Diane took Jack's diagnosis much better than I. After a day or two of crying and consulting with her mother, sisters, and friends, she picked herself up and began formulating a plan to fix our beautiful little boy.

For a while, we clung to the hope of doing just that. Thanks to a neighbor who had been through the same agonizing diagnostic process a few months before, we tracked down a number of reputable health care professionals who, more often than not, told us exactly what we wanted to hear. Or so it seemed. "No problem. Your son just needs a little extra" (pick one or more: attention, medication, speech therapy, vitamins, steroids, etc.) "and then he'll be just like every other kid." Some of these professionals even used diagnostic terms other than autism in hopes of making us feel better. My favorite was "limited multilevel systems functional cerebral noncortex disorder," or something like that.

In defense of the early experts we encountered, it's important to point out—and those of you who have been there know this—that Jack's mom and I were in a highly vulnerable state, quite open to the suggestion that our little boy would eventually be "normal."

Fill That Prescription!

"Prozac? Will that really enable me to come to terms with the fact that my son is going to probably be locked up somewhere for the rest of his life, offering absolutely nothing to himself or the world?"

My well-intentioned family doctor's suggestion that I needed something for my blossoming depression gave me hope, for about six weeks. I gave up on the mood-altering medicine because I regularly felt my skin crawling.

I went on to try Xanax, St. Johns Wort, a vegetarian diet, driving recklessly, driving carefully, regular Larry King viewing, pot, gin, beer, and Jack Daniels. Straight Jack Daniels ("neat, please") seemed to work best.

Drugs, alcohol, and other mood enhancers or depressors aside, I worked my way through those debilitating first few months thanks to the guidance of a gifted therapist, advice and counsel from close friends, empathy from Jack's two older brothers, and the joy of first-time-daughter parenting, which included soccer, basketball, soccer, softball, soccer, and more soccer.

Advances in technology helped too. A TV producer-journalist by trade, I had always wanted to create my own documentary films. Even though I owned a fairly expensive home video camera, the images it captured were hardly suitable for broadcast. During a recording session one day, a colleague showed me a brand-new Canon XL-1 digital camera. Looking through the viewfinder, I had my first ASD-related epiphany. Even though Jack wasn't in the room, I swear I saw his smiling face. Despite the fact that our family was feeling the pain of significant, uncovered medical expenses, I scraped together forty-four hundred dollars. In May 1998, the best investment I've ever made became a significant part of my dealing-and-healing process.

Through the lens of my (then state-of-the-art) recording device, I began to actually see the beauty of Jack's spirit, and, so it seemed, why he came into our world in the first place. It definitely wasn't to play baseball.

Another series of serendipitous events followed. We "discovered" Arnold Miller (Chapter Two). After serious consultation and consideration, we enrolled Jack in a summer program at the Language and Cognitive Development Center in Lynnfield, Massachusetts. During our six weeks there, thanks to two gifted teachers, Elena Bergin and Miller's wife, Eileen, Jack made astounding progress. Thankfully, most of it was recorded on videotape.

Footage in hand, I knew I had to share it with the world. A friend and colleague in Dayton, Sam Manavis, offered his video editing services for free. Together, we created an hour-long documentary called *Come Back Jack*. Jack's guitar-playing older brothers composed and performed original music for the soundtrack. A few months after completion, *Come Back Jack* aired on more than 150 public television stations in the United States, and not long after, on broadcast outlets all over the world.

An educational Website and dozens of long and short documentaries for TV and the educational marketplace followed. Requests for live presentations began pouring in. Jack was a star. Happily, I had become his mouthpiece. Sometimes I'm struck by the irony of it all. Jack, now a puberty-stricken young man with very limited expressive language capabilities, has talked to, touched, and inspired millions. I like to think my third son and fourth child knows and appreciates what he and I have been up to.

Hanging Around

Diane and I managed to stay married for a little more than seven years following Jack's ASD diagnosis, a full twenty-four months better than the "they have a special kid and their relationship has gone to hell" average. Several studies indicate that more than eight in ten families with disabled children disintegrate or experience significant difficulties within five years.

Unfortunately, for our family, the you-know-what hit the rotating device in the spring of 2000. For a myriad of reasons—nearly impossible to comprehend at the time but now ancient history (thankfully)—Diane demanded out of our twelve-year marriage.

Life is always under construction. Part of our family's construction (or deconstruction) was a divorce. Although Diane and I did a lot of good work together for Jack's benefit, our relationship was not strong enough to endure heartache, pain, confusion, stress, and financial strain.

This is not to say that Jack contributed to our breakup. He was a little boy; our problems were made by adults.

Following the contested and highly emotional legalities, despite my strong objections my now-ex-wife chose another treatment path and place of residence for my son and herself, making me a dad at a way-too-long distance since August 2001. Our daughter, Courtney, just fourteen months older than Jack, remained with me in Ohio.

Under the best of circumstances (such as living in the same house, or the same town), having a connected relationship with an ASD child is challenging. With Jack living 475 miles from his sister, Courtney, and me, it is excruciating and nearly impossible. Jack's significant expressive and receptive communication limitations exclude keeping in touch in the usual way. Our very short phone calls are a stilted, voice-hearing exercise; emailing and instant messaging are out of the question, at least for now. The less time Jack and I spend together, well, the less interested he is in having a relationship with me. I know it is not his fault. He is just more comfortable with his primary caretaker. The upside of all this is that the distance has made me more determined than ever to act as an agent for change in the ASD arena.

When it comes right down to it, that is why this book is in your hands.

Checking Out

Dozens—make that hundreds; make that thousands—of times during the Jack Parish ASD odyssey, I've been tempted to throw in the towel, get lost, disappear, give up, fly the coop, run for cover, or blast off. ASD makes parents, professionals, and caregivers crazy. It inspires vulnerability. It reaches inside the psyche, ripping at its core.

And it's exhausting.

I remember one parent telling me after a presentation, "Autism is sucking the life out of me!" I used to say to anyone who would listen, "Jack breaks my heart every day."

I often dream that Jack is typical. His age varies, but he's always old enough to play catch in the backyard after he's cut the lawn. Sometimes we're in a car together and he's driving, spitting sunflower seeds out the window into the wind.

Although we've had our moments of father-and-son ball-throwing rituals, Jack prefers throwing the glove. He will probably never be able to handle a lawnmower or operate a motor vehicle. He knows how to spit but cannot master the intricacies of separating the sunflower seed shell from the kernel. Our nondreamy interactions are complex, mostly unspoken, and certainly like nothing I have ever experienced with any human being before.

Which one of us is wrong? Which of us is right? Does it really matter? From my decade of experience, I would say most people—unless they have been blessed with an ASD child or adult in their family—do not care, to the extent we would like them to.

My parents' and sister's reactions ranged from "It's a terrible burden to carry" to "He's going to hurt someone if you don't put him away."

Like me, Jack's typical older brothers and sister love him from a distance. Graham and Ryan both work with children, teenagers, and young adults with issues ranging from ASD to substance abuse. Courtney talks about becoming a psychologist. Diane, still on the front lines, has embarked toward a career as a special education teacher. Her parents have been generous with financial support. ASD interventions can be frightfully expensive and are not usually covered by health insurance. But other relatives, on all branches of the family tree, have kept their distance, and sadly this is often the norm.

There is something disturbing about ASD, and how even the most loving and compassionate react to it. My friend (and Jack's former developmental pediatrician) Dr. Patty Manning, the director of the Kelly O'Leary Center for ASD at Children's Hospital Medical Center in Cincinnati, once told me that ASD children and adults strike fear in the hearts of others because, in general, every society has a hard time understanding "a child who doesn't connect."

Blessed Are the "Angels"

Certainly one of the most profound learnings from what I sometimes call the "Jack Attack" is that there are people—sometimes professionals, sometimes not—who truly have a gift of connecting joyfully with this population of children and adults.

Angie Porter, Jack's first private therapist, began working with him in August 1997. She was a third-year occupational therapy student at Xavier University in Cincinnati. Despite her training, Jack scared her at first. He was, in fact, the first person with ASD she had ever met. We asked Angie, and all of Jack's "angels" (as we called our freelance helpers), to keep a journal about their experience. What she wrote about her first few encounters with my son is definitely worth sharing:

> I have to say that I was definitely intimidated upon first impressions. I was so shy and soft-spoken that I thought that Jack would probably eat me alive! Here was this little boy bouncing off of the walls and not really giving two hoots about who I was, or why I was there. When I realized I could help make a difference in Jack's life, that was what really made me jump right in and get over my quietness.

Off and on for more than three years, Angie jumped, hugged, connected, and accepted. Their time together wasn't always a walk in the park. But like the rest of us, she reveled in his accomplishments.

Another Angie journal entry:

> One of the biggest breakthroughs I saw was in the swimming pool. At the beginning of the summer, Jack liked getting in the water as long as he could touch the bottom and did not have to go under. What little swimming he did was the doggie-paddle. His swimming instructor in-sisted that all of the kids go under at least once while in the pool. This would be the worst for me. Jack would get so mad at me for pushing him under. It got to the point that Jack did not even want to get in the pool anymore. He would scream and cry the whole time we were in the water. I worked so hard to build his trust in me so he would know that I would not let him get hurt. One day we were in the shallow end of the pool and we were making bubbles in the water. Jack loved to

watch the bubbles rise to the top. All of a sudden, I saw Jack's little head go under. I waited, and up he popped with a huge smile on his face! Within just a few weeks, Jack was swimming underwater, jumping into the deep end, and eventually flying off of the diving board.

All of Jack's angels were young women in their early twenties. More often than not, they were special education students from local universities. His longest-lasting, and perhaps most important, early educational influence was a young woman already working in a classroom. When we met Theresa Mitchell, she was the lead preschool teacher at an amazing place called Stepping Stones Center, a nonprofit facility in Cincinnati that serves disabled children and adults.

Theresa's connection with Jack was immediate and profound. Watching her work with him in a nonhome environment began giving me a true appreciation for the dedication, discipline, and caring that it takes to succeed, to excel as a teacher for ASD children.

Jack's mom and I were so impressed with Theresa's innate talent that we made a pitch for her to become Jack's full-time aide when he began his public school journey. After some serious negotiating with both Stepping Stones and our school district, Theresa began working full-time with him. She was his transportation coordinator, playground buddy, and constant learning companion.

Her journal entries were always heartfelt and revealing. One of her first, not long after they began first grade together, was especially touching:

Well, now it's Jack and I. We have begun this journey into the realm of public school together, as a team. You could say we're like two cyclists on a bicycle built for two. We are slowly, but surely pedaling ahead. Occasionally, we fall, but we get back up and try again. Some days we climb mountains with ease. These days touch me in such a profound way. To see Jack run and play, hand in hand, with other children, smiling and looking into their eyes, or to hear him use language that knocks me off my feet is so undoubtedly rewarding. While, I know that some days Jack wishes I would do all the pedaling, he also knows that I won't because I care (tough love, kiddo—I'm on your side!).

I see Jack's future clearly. The day will come when he no longer needs me. He'll hop on his bicycle built for one, his legs pumping away, his eyes bright and alive, with that famous Jack smile on his face, he'll ride off all on his own. I never realized all of the simple things in life that I was missing out on until I met Jack. I never knew how neat the ripples in the water are when you throw something into it. I never stopped to watch how dust sparkles when you throw it into the sunlight. I have learned a lot about myself, thanks to Jack too. I never knew I had so much patience, first of all. I also never knew I could be so stern and strict. Thank you Jack—for making my life even better than it already was.

Thankfully, there have been dozens of gifted educators who have followed in Angie and Theresa's footsteps. All who have accomplished the sometimes-daunting task of connecting with my son share many of the same inherent or learned qualities. Willingness to learn from another human being who many, or perhaps even most, view as impaired is one such trait. Tossing out preconceived notions about typical interactions can be a great place to start.

Once I picked up my video camera and stopped attempting to engage Jack in the same way I did my other children—or just about anyone else I had ever met, for that matter—that was when I started to feel more comfortable with who my son actually was. Shock! In turn, he began to feel more comfortable with me.

Through the lens, my preconceptions were trashed; the myths about autism began to shatter before my eyes. I was able to really pay attention and pick up on opportunities to engage, even if it was something I had never done before.

I'll Have Fries with That (Part One)

Christmas afternoon. In the car with Courtney and Jack. Not the best day for my youngest son. He'd arrived at my house with an old Windows-based computer game ("Freddie the Fish") that would not play on any of my Macintosh devices. To say the least, he was very unhappy with this turn of events.

Santa Claus was generous with Jack, but he was not interested in any of the unique presents under our tree. The only solution to his nerve-wracking holiday meltdown was a long ride in the car. Thankfully, or so I thought, "Freddie the Fish. Freddie the Fish" was quickly replaced by "French Fries. Chocolate Milk. French Fries. Chocolate Milk." There is something about getting in the car that inspires Jack's salivary glands and hunger pangs to activate, even if he has eaten recently.

Wendy's has long been his favorite.

Most of us have the ability to immediately process and accept when it's not possible to partake in a fabulous fast-food meal. December 25 may be the only time Wendy's drive-thru is not available. Who doesn't know that? Jack didn't. Despite the best efforts of Courtney and me, no amount of explanation was going to enlighten him. My son needed to experience, up close and personal, why his Christmas wish could not be granted. I drove to Jack's perseveration inspiration. Pulling into Wendy's driveway, I stopped abruptly at the Place Your Order Here speaker.

I sat quietly. Jack waited in great anticipation. After about a minute, I said with a very enthusiastic affect, "Hey. Is anybody in there?" Of course, there was no response. Next, I tapped on the speaker box, my voice rising in feigned irritation. "C'mon; we're hungry out here. Where is everybody?"

I glanced in the rear view mirror, and noticed Jack was being very attentive to my antics. Since he was connecting with the proceedings, I decided to ramp it up a fry or two. I whapped the box, accentuating the sound with a verbal effect of my own, and demanded answers. "I know you're in there. I don't care if it's Christmas Day. My son Jack wants french fries and chocolate milk. This is just not right! You're ruining his Christmas!"

I turned to Jack and said, "I can't believe this, can you? Have you ever seen such a thing?"

Jack waved his right hand, encouraging me to pull forward to the window. I did. No one greeted us. It was dark inside. My one last bit of drama was to tap on the window, again imploring anyone with french-frying ability to step forward and grant our request. I took a deep breath, turned to my son, and said, "It looks like Wendy's is closed today. I guess everyone who usually works here is home celebrating Christmas. We'll try again tomorrow, when they're open." Courtney, attempting to control her laughter, echoed my sentiments.

Jack smiled. To my surprise and delight, he said, "Potato chips, please!" He had noticed, moments before, when we passed the parking lot of a neighborhood convenience store, that the lights there were on and people were inside buying things.

I pulled into the parking lot, grinning from ear to ear. Dashing inside, I grabbed three bags, including Jack's favorite (salt and vinegar). Despite bursting with pride, I resisted the temptation of telling the sad woman behind the cash register that my son just had a "breakthrough moment."

When Jack and I share experiences like this, I often wonder what the mythical fly on the wall would think. Over the years, even though I sometimes battle my own inhibitions, I've come to realize that when he and I are together it is vitally important for me to pitch concerns about audience reaction and be totally in the moment.

How others judge our interactions in public (so long as they are in the socially appropriate ballpark) is irrelevant. More often than not, our antics provide a teachable moment.

I'll Have Fries with That (Part Two)

Jack's most intense Mount St. Helens meltdowns always seem to occur in a store called bigg's. (I have no explanation for the lower case, but it is the official spelling.) bigg's is the southwest Ohio version of Wal-Mart. Inside, they stock everything from vegetables to videotapes. Jack has a love-hate relationship with bigg's (so do I, but we save a lot of money shopping there), and for us to pay a visit I really have to be in the zone, or have help from one of Jack's siblings.

A few years ago, all my boys were roaming the aisles with me. Jack, who despite his size still loves to ride in the shopping cart, was most interested in the entertainment section, which had shelves upon shelves of VHS tapes featuring Winnie the Pooh in every possible video incarnation. For the record, I have never enjoyed Christopher Robin, Rabbit, Owl, or most of their friends. With the exception of Tigger, my personal belief is that most of these animated characters should be relegated into a honeycomb-laden space capsule and launched into the farthest reaches of our solar system.

God bless my youngest son. For whatever reason, he believes the sun shines and sets on the inhabitants of the Hundred Acre Wood. On this particular bigg's visit, I decided to assert my authority. We passed the entertainment section, and Jack began his perseveration: "Winnie the Pooh. Winnie the Pooh." I responded with, "Not today, Jack. We're here to buy food, including your favorite: french fries."

It was not the best statement I have ever made. Jack looked at me with his big blue eyes and started crying: "Winnie the Pooh, Dad. Winnie the Pooh." I remained steadfast, even though Jack's older brothers and every shopper within whispering distance were engrossed in our earsplitting interaction.

We reached the checkout line, with just a few grocery items in our cart. Jack continued, gaining volume and momentum every second: "Winnie the Pooh. Winnie the Pooh." I just shook my head. Graham and Ryan had seen their father's stubbornness before. But even they were taken aback by their little brother's volatility.

"Winnie the Pooh. Winnie the Pooh." Our friendly bigg's customer service person was more than a bit disturbed. I finally asked my older typical boys to take their vociferous little brother to our car. As the boys left the building, Jack's perseveration echoed throughout the shopping center. It made most within earshot (everyone!) very uncomfortable.

After I paid for our food, I was surrounded (or so it seemed) by dozens of curious onlookers in dire need of an explanation. Part of me wanted to tell them all to get a life (I was no longer in the zone). I collected myself and said, "My son has autism. His brain doesn't always process events the way ours do. And sometimes when he doesn't get what he wants, he gets very loud and upset." My bigg's audience seemed mostly satisfied with my explanation. All but the cashier and a toothless grandma returned to their preoutburst tasks. I began placing our bounty in plastic bags.

The well-meaning checkout lady said, "I am so sorry. It must be difficult for you and your family." I responded by telling her, "Autism makes life interesting, that's for sure, But my son teaches us so much." She smiled in disbelief and moved on to the next customer.

The grandma, who for some inexplicable reason was holding a tube of toothpaste, looked at me quite seriously and said, "That's such a relief; I thought your little boy was being kidnapped." I assured her that everything was all right, and he was in good hands.

As if to prove my point, when I arrived at the car my three boys were inside immersed in what I like to call a "rough and tumble tickle-fest." Jack had moved on from yearning for the animated antics of Winnie the Pooh to real-live human-to-human contact. I lifted the hatchback, placed the three plastic grocery bags in the car, and stood there in awe, watching Jack and his big brothers connect.

Hundreds of times during the past decade or more, difficult moments, which sometimes seem like hours, have turned on a dime—or in this case, a pot of honey—mostly because those of us closest to Jack realize that his outbursts, meltdowns, or whatever we choose to call them at the time are temporary and, when it comes right down to it, understandable.

Slow Down and Breathe

Reveling in small accomplishments. Embracing miniscule miracles that take serious squinting to see clearly. Turning away the darkness of typical expectations. Enthusiastic discovering, even when it appears there is nothing to learn. Being present when your ASD companion is off in the distance, right in front of you. As parents of and advocates for ASD kids, that's what we do. The educators who have a gift for connecting with these children are right there with us.

Learning how to connect with ASD children is, in my view, a different way of being. When Jack and I are at our best together, he has a little something to do with it. But, mostly, it's up to me.

Mostly, I don't mind at all.

What Next? What If?

Now that Jack is in his teenage years, and we have a solid perspective about his cognitive, social, and behavioral limitations, I've forced myself to face what some would consider a number of harsh realities. Barring a major scientific breakthrough, unforeseen miracle, or planetary realignment, my youngest son will probably never:

Cut the lawn

Drive a car

Cram for the SATs

Join a high school debating team

Participate in typical team sports

Make out with a date in a dark movie theater

Bug me for an allowance

Live independently

Bless me with grandchildren

There are, of course, dozens or hundreds more of the "probably-nevers." But I could create a similar list, describing not only me ("Robert will never dress in a stylish manner") but all my children and everyone else I know well.

No matter how at peace I am with this ASD thing, I am certain I will always crave a "real" conversation with Jack. I sometimes daydream about him and me sitting on the dock of the bay, exchanging witty commentary about whatever comes to mind. I really believe I have a good idea of what Jack would say to me if he could say it. Luckily, I guess, I am more right-than left-brained, which means my creative side is strong. Plus I've been told during my thirty-some years in the media business that I'm very adept at writing dialogue.

So, with a little imagination, I will guess that if young Jack had conversational, expressive language skills, our banter might go something like this:

Dad: How are you doing today?

Jack: Just being myself.

Dad: I have to know. What's it like?

Jack: What's what like?

Dad: Autism.

Jack: I'm not sure what you mean.

Dad: You know, that disability you have—autism spectrum disorder, or ASD.

Jack: Disability? Sorry, I don't understand the concept.

Dad: You know, the difference in your brain that keeps you from living a full, meaningful, independent life.

Jack: My life is meaningful. I'm fine.

Dad: What makes you say that?

Jack: I'm not exactly sure. I do know I am who I am. You know. Me.

Dad: Right. But don't you feel different from most other people?

Jack: I don't really know how other people feel.

Dad: What about the way people look at you sometimes? For instance, when you're making those "meltdown" sounds of yours in the grocery store.

Jack: I don't really notice.

Dad: You don't notice?

Jack: I guess some people look scared, but I don't blame them.

Dad: Why not?

Jack: This world can be a scary place.

Dad: So, what are you afraid of?

Jack: Well, I'm not so crazy about buzzing hair clippers or loud noises.

Dad: What else?

Jack: I don't know. I really haven't given that question much thought. I know it when I see or hear it.

Dad: Do you worry about your future?

Jack: No. Should I?

Dad: Most people do.

Jack: I'm not most people.

Dad: So, you like who you are?

Jack: Of course. Don't you?

Dad: No, I don't like myself all the time.

Jack: Why not?

Dad: Probably because I don't have to.

Jack: You don't have to? I don't get that at all.

Dad: Neither do I.

Jack: Are you trying to change me?

Dad: Not anymore.

Jack: You mean, you wanted to before?

Dad: Yes, I wanted you to be more like me.

Jack: But I'm not you.

Dad: I know.

Jack: I'm me, and have never been anyone else.

Dad: I imagine that's the way it's going to stay.

Jack: I bet you're right.

Dad: Are you hungry?

Jack: Of course. French fries, please.

14

THE BIG QUESTION

(After receiving, reviewing, and discussing all the chapters, I returned to all the contributors and asked what I call the "big question." —RP)

Question

What, in your view, is the most important concept for professional educators to embrace in interacting with ASD children and adults?

Answers

Diane Bayer: It is one of the most awesome jobs to teach and to help those who have disabilities. I know, because I was an educator for many years. Now, as a parent of a child in the autism spectrum, I have even more respect for those who wish to teach or provide therapy to this population. This is not an easy job by any stretch of the imagination, yet the rewards are immeasurable. One of the things I understand more clearly now, from a parental perspective, is that the person who stands before you "in need" of your help is so much more than a number on a chart or a diagnosis. What the psychiatric label or diagnosis does not tell you is that this is a person who is loved by someone. This person is someone's child, someone's brother or sister, someone's cousin, someone's friend. This individual before you is unique and cherished. The charts and labels and behavioral rating scales cannot ever tell you who this person is or who he or she will become.

I would implore anyone working in the field providing services to those in the autism spectrum to look beyond the label and take the time to get to know the person you are serving. People with autism are not outcome studies in the making. They are people first, with their own wants, needs, and dreams for the future. If this were your child, grandchild, sibling, or friend before you, how would you teach or help? The person you are serving will be your guide and your teacher. Allow yourself to be open to the possibilities inherent in developing a relationship with those you serve. It is only through this relationship that true growth and learning will take root and finally blossom.

Robert Becerra: The most important concept is respect. Respect for persons with autism, their differences and uniqueness. All therapies and instruction should be done carefully with this in mind, so that their spirit isn't crushed in an effort to get them to conform to what we call normal. Kindness, gentleness, and patience are the hallmarks of respect, and they should inform every interaction.

Teresa Becerra: When we talk about theories, methods, ideas, concepts, it's with the understanding that once those things are mastered you have someone who is then trained and qualified to work in the field of study. But when we talk about someone who is going to work with children with autism, we're talking about more than just qualifications for a job. I don't think that it's just a matter of learning techniques or concepts as much as I think it's a matter of intuition, instinct, and nature.

I think anyone can learn to work with a child who has autism, and probably be successful in many ways, especially if he or she spends enough time learning, observing, and practicing; but it's more than that. I'm sure you've heard people say that it takes a special person to work with special children. To me, when I see an educator or therapist who has the gift, I know the person didn't learn it from a book. When you watch a true master work with a child who has autism, you see an artist who loves what she is doing and doesn't even know she is creating a masterpiece. It's a rare and wonderful gift, especially to those children who are lucky enough to be on the other side.

My best advice to an educator who really wants to stand out, who really has a huge passion, who really wants to make a difference, is to do a little reading outside of the field. Go and study the work of Jane Goodall, and Monty Roberts (the Horse Whisperer). Their ideas, methods, techniques, and concepts are the same. They have an understanding of the sacredness of the world they have entered. They have enormous respect for the soul. They know instinctively what's right and what's wrong. They dare not enter until the moment is right, no matter how long the moment takes. They don't have an agenda. They have the time. They know how important it is to form a bond first, because they know how important the trust factor is. They know how to wait for the teachable moment, because they know how to be the student first. They're at peace with the entire process, and they don't find the need to rush it in any way. I think a good way to describe it would be "the art of autism," because it is a fine art. These individuals are such gifts to our children, and as parents we are forever grateful.

Kristina Chew: Embrace the notion of "presuming competence"—understanding that a special ed child has ability and intelligence but does not always show them in the typical ways. Understand that if a child is not learning, a teacher needs to look at her or his teaching methods, style, and so forth and access what is working and what is not. (I write this from my own experiences teaching, too).

Gay and Dennis Debbaudt: For safety's sake, discover and then anticipate the consequences of your actions and those of the person with ASD. Be (or become) a mind reader.

Kristin Kaifas-Tennyson: One of the most important concepts to remember is that behavior is language, and it is our job to figure out what our kids are trying to tell or communicate to us. Behavior often functions as language for ASD kids because they are unable to communicate their needs.

This could be due to the fact that the child is nonverbal or has a processing issue, or it could even be a very bright child who loses the ability to communicate once he becomes overwhelmed or frustrated. Then our kids learn to communicate through behavior, and this can become a learned response. For example, if a child cannot speak, she may go over to the shelf where the pop is kept and start crying. Eventually, mom or dad (by trial and error) will start asking questions. "Do you want the crackers? Do you want the pop?" Once they hit the right question, the child's needs are met and the child learns that crying by the shelves is a way of communicating "I'd like some pop, please!"

Jeanne Lyons: Some professional educators have worked successfully with my son Shawn, but others have not. The ones who have helped him believed in his sensory differences and helped him understand and manage them. They understood that behavior modification techniques are no match for sensory issues and fixations.

They struck a balance between being structured and flexible, providing structure without being rigid.

They saw my son as an individual, with gifts and deficits. Finally, they were respectful to Shawn and demonstrated this respectful attitude in front of his classmates. Because they decided to be intrigued by him instead of annoyed, his classmates were also intrigued and not annoyed.

Jackie Marquette: I think it is highly significant that school personnel and other professionals closely consider a variety of personal supports that can facilitate the student's participation in learning or joining a group. His or her participation may only be willingness at first. If so, I would suggest that educators recognize even willingness as a step toward success. Practice looking from the student's perspective.

Cammie McGovern: I have loved and appreciated the teachers who bravely pushed past my son's early resistance to all learning and being presented with new and challenging material. It is exhausting and no doubt very hard to see the gains when they happen so slowly over the course of a year. But parents see them and years after the fact remember those early, extraordinary teachers in the preschool and kindergarten years and wish there was a way to express their gratitude. Now that my son is in fourth grade and integrated into a mainstream classroom with much support, I am especially grateful for the regular ed teachers who take time to find creative ways for my son to interact with his peers successfully. I also love anyone who sees the humor in the countless odd things ASD children do and say. They remind us daily that these kids can be really funny.

Arnold Miller: Educators need to consistently distinguish between the appearance of meaningful functioning and its actual substance. They need to challenge the notion that "if it quacks like a duck and walks like a duck, it is a duck." We have seen far too many special children and adults who seem to be acting appropriately, using perfectly articulated speech, or "reading," without having a clue as to what they are doing, saying, or reading (to accept the duck simile). The special educator—and, for that matter, all who work with special children—must be from Missouri ("Show me!") until the children clearly demonstrate their understanding.

Robert Parish: It's very important to be totally open to possibilities. Avoid judgment. Follow your instincts, and your heart. Don't be afraid to throw out what you think you know or have learned. Go with the flow. Feel the energy. Get in the zone. Connecting with these children is a sometimes-challenging process. Never take anything personally. Love unconditionally.

Susan Senator: Most important, professional educators need to try to understand that this is a person they are dealing with, not a creature, not a set of behaviors, but a person who—though differently wired—thinks and feels like anyone else.

Stephen Shore: Find ways for people with autism to use their strengths to achieve success—just like everyone else.

Kim Stagliano: The general special education tools of ten or more years ago are not sufficient to teach the autism population. I would ask teachers to push for districtwide autism training for all staff, including therapists and paraprofessionals. The difference for our kids is astounding.

[RESOURCES]

Editor's note: Our collective goal with this book is to connect professionals and parents with thoughtful and thorough information about ASD.

Every contributor made suggestions for the list that follows. Obviously, our preferences are not all-inclusive. Thanks primarily to the Internet and the fact that autism is finally getting the attention it deserves, new information is published every day. Hopefully, through our list, you'll discover a printed or electronic perspective about autism that you can embrace as we have.

Nonfiction

1001 Great Ideas for Teaching and Raising Children with Autism Spectrum Disorders, by Ellen Notbohm and Veronica Zysk (Future Horizons, 2004)

Asperger's Syndrome: A Guide for Parents and Professionals, by Tony Attwood (Jessica Kingsley, 1998)

Asperger's Syndrome and Self-Esteem, by Norm Ledgin (Future Horizons, 2000)

The Autism Acceptance Book: Being a Friend to Someone with Autism, by Ellen Sabin (Watering Can, 2006)

Autism and the Metaphor of the Person Alone, by Douglas Biklen (New York University Press, 2005)

Autism for Dummies, by Stephen Shore and Linda Rastelli (Wiley, 2006)

Autism Heroes, by Barbara Firestone (Jessica Kingsley, 2007)

Becoming Remarkably Able: Walking the Path to Independence and Beyond, by Jackie Marquette (Marquette Group, 2007)

Beyond the Wall: Personal Experiences with Autism, by Stephen Shore (Autism Asperger, 2000)

Classic Readings in Autism, by Anne Donnellan (Teachers College Press, 1985)

Genius Genes, by Michael Fitzgerald and Brendan O'Brien (Autism Asperger, 2007)

Let Me Hear Your Voice: A Family's Triumph over Autism, by Catherine Maurice (Fawcett Columbia, 1993)

Look Me in the Eye, by John Elder Robison (Random House, 2007)

Louder than Words, by Jenny McCarthy (Dutton, 2007)

Making Peace with Autism, by Susan Senator (Trumpeter Books, 2005)

The Miller Method: Developing the Capacities of Children on the Autism Spectrum, by Arnold Miller with Kristina Chretien (Jessica Kingsley, 2006)

More Than Words, by Fern Sussman (Hanen Centre, 1999)

The Original Social Story Book, by Carol Gray (Future Horizons, 1993)

Send in the Idiots: Growing Up in Another World, by Kamran Nazeer (Bloomsbury, 2006)

The Siege, by Clara Clairborne Park (Little, Brown, 1967)

A Slant of Sun: One Child's Courage, by Beth Kephart (Norton, 1998)

Ten Things Your Student with Autism Wishes You Knew, by Ellen Notbohm (Future Horizons, 2004)

There's a Boy in Here, by Judy Barron and Sean Barron (Chapmans, 1993)

Thinking in Pictures and Other Reports of My Life with Autism, by Temple Grandin (Bantam, 1995)

Understanding and Working with the Spectrum of Autism: An Insider's View, by Wendy Lawson (Jessica Kingsley, 2001)

Unstrange Minds, by Roy Richard Grinker (Basic Books, 2007)

Fiction

The Curious Case of the Dog in the Nighttime, by Mark Haddon (Random House, 2003)

Daniel Isn't Talking, by Marti Leimbach (Anchor, 2007)

Eye Contact, by Cammie McGovern (Viking, 2006)

Family Pictures: A Novel, by Sue Miller (Harper, 1999)

Fire Stone, by V. C. Keating (Trafford, 2006)

Gold of the Sunbeams and Other Stories, by Soma and Tito Mukhopadhyay (Arcade, 2005)

Stonking Steps, by Will Rogers (Trafford, 2006)

Taking Care of Cleo, by Bill Broder (Handsel, 2006)

Urville, by Giles Trehin (Jessica Kingsley, 2006)

Wild Orchid, by Beverly Brenna (Red Deer, 2006)

A Wild Ride up the Cupboards, by Ann Bauer (Scribner, 2005)

Internet

Aspires (www.aspires-relationships.com)

Autism Hub (www.autismhub.com)

Autism One (www.autismone.org)

Autism Press (www.autismpress.com)

Autism Society of America (www.autism-society.org)

Autism Speaks (www.autismspeaks.org)

Autism Vox (www.autismvox.com)

Barbara Fischkin (www.barbarafischkin.com)

Cammie McGovern's Website (www.cammiemcgovern.com)

Council for Exceptional Children (www.cec.sped.org)

Dennis Debbaudt's Website (www.autismriskmanagement.com)

Diane Bayer's Website (www.theautismexpress.com)

FEAT (www.feat.org)

First Signs (www.firstsigns.org)

Jackie Marquette's Website (www.independencebound.com)

Jeanne Lyons's Website (www.lyonstunes.com)

Jeff's Life (www.jeffslife.net)

Kim Stagliano's blog (www.kimstagliano.blogspot.com)

Kristina Chew's Websites (www.kristinachew.com) (www.autismvox.com)

The Miller Method (www.millermethod.org)

My Life as an Autistic Boy (http://users.adelphia.net/~d.priebe/)

National Autism Association (www.nationalautismassociation.org)

Neurodiversity (www.neurodiversity.com)

Paula Kluth (www.paulakluth.com)

Postively Autism (www.positivelyautism.com)

Program Development Associates (www.pdasoc.com)

Rescue Post (www.rescuepost.com)

Robert Parish/Come Back Jack (www.comebackjack.org)

Savage Records (www.savagerecords.com)

Shafer Autism Report (www.sarnet.org)

The Special Needs Project (www.specialneeds.com)

Stephen Shore's Website (www.autismasperger.net)

Susan Senator's Website (www.susansenator.com)

Temple Grandin (www.templegrandin.com)

University of Miami (www.umcard.org)

Unlocking Autism (www.unlockingautism.org)

Theatrical Films

Being There (United Artists, 1979)

The Boy Who Could Fly (20th Century Fox, 1986)

Forrest Gump (Paramount, 1994)

House of Cards (Miramax, 1993)

Mercury Rising (Imagine Entertainment, 1998)

Rain Man (MGM/UA, 1988)

Snowcake (Revolution Films, 2006)

What's Eating Gilbert Grape (Paramount Pictures, 1993)

Documentary Films

Autism Every Day (October Group/Milestone Video, 2006)

Autism Is a World (CNN, 2004)

Autism: Oh, the Possibilities (KVCR, 2006)

Autism: The Musical (BMP Films, 2007)

The Autism Puzzle (BBC, 2005)

Autism: The Musical (Bunim-Murray/Effect Films, 2007)

Children with Autism: One Teacher's Experience (Model Me Kids, 2007)

Come Back Jack (Write Field Features, 1998)

The Hope and Heartache of Autism (Northwestern University, 2005)

Mirror Mind (Daniel Wee, 2006)

Normal People Scare Me (Normal Films, 2006)

Refrigerator Mothers (PBS, 2004)

Riding Shotgun with ASD (Write Field Features, 2007)

Without Apology (One-eyed Cat Productions, 2004)

[INDEX]